BACKPACKING

AROUND THE WORLD

A Guide to Independent and Safe Travel

(half the cost, twice the fun)

BILL PASSMAN

"*I sought to see the amazing as normal, and the daily as unique, and in that swirling paradox I found the joy of travel.*"

Mary Poxon

This book is dedicated to my mother, Virginia Hanks Passman, who taught me to live life with passion.

The Greeks never wrote obituaries, they only asked one question. "Did they live their life with passion?"

🌺

And to my dad, Charley Fred Passman, who taught me that material things are not the most important thing in the world.

"To have what we want is riches, but to be able to do without is power.

Donald Grant

🌺

This combination led me to backpacking around the world.

🌺

CONTENTS

Introduction   *xi*

Chapter 1
What is Backpacking?   *1*

Chapter 2
What are Hostels?   *13*

Chapter 3
Why Travel?   *25*

Chapter 4
Traveling Solo or With Someone   *37*

Chapter 5
Travel Guides (the backpacker's encyclopedia)   *49*

Chapter 6
Where, When and How Long to Travel   *57*

Chapter 7
Passports and Visas   *69*

Chapter 8
Planning the Trip   *75*

Chapter 9
Packing   *93*

Chapter 10
Traveling   *109*

Chapter 11
Being a Good Traveler   *145*

Chapter 12
Coming Home   *149*

Acknowledgement

To my brother, Morgan, for inspiring me with his stories of backpacking through Europe and my sons (Scott, Beau, and Jon), grandchildren (Kade and Madison) and daughter-in-law (Amber) who give me a reason to come back from each journey.

INTRODUCTION

----

his book began as something to do when I was unable to travel during 2009. When backpackers are not able to travel, they like to talk about travel. Since I was unable to travel or find anyone who wanted to talk about travel, I decided to write about travel. When I began backpacking in 2006, I was unable to find any How-To books on backpacking and had to rely on travel guides, travel blogs and the internet for my source of backpacking knowledge. Backpacking around the world became my passion. When not traveling the world, I was researching every aspect of backpacking so that I could travel more inexpensively. I became a self-appointed ambassador for backpacking and tried at every opportunity to convince others to try backpacking as an alternative to the traditional vacation. It was this desire to share my passion for backpacking that led me to write this book. I hope that this will make it a little easier for those who are interested in learning about backpacking as a way of travel. This book provides enough information to give the novice backpacker a foundation from which to plan and complete their backpacking journey. My intent was to provide this information in as compact form as possible without adding unneeded information just to fill pages. Unfortunately, many things just have to be learned on the road. That is why it is called independent travel and that is what makes it so exciting.

This book was written mostly for the majority of Americans, especially mature travelers, who have little or no understanding of backpacking. Most Americans think that backpacking involves lots of walking and carrying an enormous backpack. I am hopeful this book will provide a better understanding of backpacking and show its many advantages and rewards. The most difficult backpacking obstacle for Americans is the concept of traveling for extended periods. While those in Europe have paid vacations for six to eight weeks, most Americans consider one to two weeks the maximum time they could take off from work. Hopefully, one day, employees and employers will adopt less restrictive vacation/travel time. Until that day, those who have not yet begun their careers and those who have retired or semi-retired will have to carry on the backpacking tradition for Americans. Those who are unable to get additional vacation/travel time should try backpacking with whatever time they can squeeze out of their hectic work schedules. A few backpacking trips will lead to an earnest effort to try to increase their time off from work. I think it would be great if one day Americans were afforded the same vacation/travel time as those in Europe, at least from a backpacking perspective.

"LIFE IS NOT MEASURED BY THE NUMBER OF BREATHS WE TAKE BUT BY THE PLACES AND MOMENTS THAT TAKE OUR BREATH AWAY."

Anonymous

WHAT IS BACKPACKING?

PUBLIC TRANSPORTATION

The use of public transportation is an important tool for backpackers due to its inexpensive cost. Public transportation includes planes, trains, buses, boats, shuttles, subways, taxis, bikes and walking. Costs are usually very low in comparison to a guided tour or rental car and allows for interaction with the locals. In many cities, special passes offer discounts for local transportation. It also eliminates the difficulties of driving a car in a foreign country and the expenses such as car rental, fuel, insurance and parking which can be difficult to find and costly.

YOUTH HOSTELS

Hostels, formally called youth hostels, provide inexpensive lodging and services geared for the independent traveler. Whether you choose to stay in a dorm or private room, there is no mistaking the sense of adventure and excitement of staying in a hostel. The services provided by hostels are almost as important as the low cost sleeping accommodations. These are explained in detail in the chapter "WHAT ARE HOSTELS?" Hostels, however, are not the only places that back-packers stay. Family guesthouses and budget hotels are sometimes very inexpensive and provide a great alternative when hostels are not available.

LENGTH OF TRIP

Traveling inexpensively and without the re-strictions of a guided tour itinerary allows one to travel for a longer period. This allows the backpacker to move at a slower pace (which is less expensive), use local transportation and make changes to your plans based on circumstances, knowledge acquired or whims. Guided tours do not allow the freedom to search out the best "off the road" sights listed in travel guides. You will stumble upon many unknown spots when you have time to travel at your own pace.

> "A GOOD TRAVELER HAS NO FIXED PLANS AND IS NOT INTENT ON ARRIVING."
> *Lao Tzu*

USE OF BACKPACK

The use of a backpack is another essential element of backpacking and immediately distinguishes a backpacker from a traditional tourist. A backpack allows the freedom needed to travel quickly and effortlessly without worrying about packing and keeping up with lots of luggage. If making one or more connecting flights, you will appreciate not having to worry about lost luggage by only having a carry-on backpack. Backpacks have evolved greatly. They are lightweight, sturdy and come in many different sizes with lots of compartments. Some hybrids are equipped with rollers so you can pull them behind you or use them in the traditional fashion. It is not necessary to bring your entire wardrobe on the trip. Believe it or not, other countries have laundry facilities, clothing stores and places to buy toiletries, if needed. With today's hefty airline baggage fees, it is essential to pack light and use carry-on luggage to reduce costs.

> "OWN ONLY WHAT YOU CAN CARRY WITH
> YOU; KNOW LANGUAGE, KNOW COUNTRIES, KNOW
> PEOPLE. LET YOUR MEMORY BE YOUR TRAVEL BAG."
> *Alexander Solzhenitsyn*

INTERACTION WITH LOCALS

An important distinction between backpackers and traditional tourists is their desire to interact with the locals and learn about their culture. Traditional guided tours usually consist of being picked up at the airport, driven to your hotel, picked up at the hotel by a tour bus, driven to the tourist sights, back to the hotel and then to the airport at the end of the trip. If spending your time with the same tourists at the hotel and on the tour bus is your idea of travel, then backpacking is not for you.

There is nothing more exciting than riding a local bus, eating in one of the night markets or local (not tourist) restaurants, shopping in the farmer's market or just exploring the city or village on your own. After seeing the main tourist sights, I always like to spend a few days observing, talking to locals, learning about the culture and trying my best to fit in. A few words in the local language and a smile go a long way in showing your appreciation to the locals for allowing you to visit their country. Traveling is so much more than just seeing the tourist sights.

> "IF YOU REJECT THE FOOD, IGNORE THE CUSTOMS, FEAR THE RELIGION AND AVOID THE PEOPLE, YOU MIGHT BETTER STAY HOME."
>
> *James Michener*

SEEING THE SIGHTS

While climbing Mount Everest, Tenzig Norgay told Sir Edmund Hillary, "Some people come to look, while others come to see."

Mount Everest, Nepal

To me that truly explains the difference between backpackers and traditional tourists. So many tourists are interested in getting that "one photo" of each traditional tourist sight to share with family and friends. Backpackers are also interested in the everyday life that surrounds that tourist sight. The backpacker is not limited by the time constraints and structure of the guided tour and has freedom to explore. While gazing over Machu Picchu for the first time, you should not have to worry about the guide telling you that it is time to board the bus. If you have the time to search, you may discover many little known, inexpensive places and activities known only by the locals. Information from hostels and other backpackers lead to incredible "off the path" sights and activities that are not listed in most guidebooks. Sometimes exploring unknown streets and places can lead to the most astounding finds.

"ALL JOURNEYS HAVE SECRET DESTINATIONS OF WHICH THE TRAVELER IS UNAWARE."
Martin Buber

Machu Picchu, Peru

"TOURISTS DON'T KNOW WHERE THEY'VE BEEN,
TRAVELERS DON'T KNOW WHERE THEY'RE GOING."
Paul Theroux

STATE OF MIND

- -

From Wikipedia, the free encyclopedia

"OF IMPORTANCE IN BACKPACKING IS A SENSE OF
AUTHENTICITY. BACKPACKING IS PERCEIVED AS
BEING MORE THAN A VACATION, BUT A MEANS OF
EDUCATION. BACKPACKERS WANT TO EXPERIENCE
THE "REAL" DESTINATION RATHER THAN THE
PACKAGED VERSION OFTEN ASSOCIATED WITH
MASS TOURISM, WHICH HAS LED TO THE ASSERTION
THAT BACKPACKERS ARE ANTI-TOURISTS. THERE IS
ALSO THE FEELING OF "SNEAKING BACKSTAGE" AND
WITNESSING REAL LIFE WITH MORE INVOLVEMENT
WITH LOCAL PEOPLE."

Backpacking is a state of mind that evolves into a way of life. Backpackers do not go on vacation; they travel. The pursuit of new experiences, sights, knowledge and friends seem more like an addiction at times.

"THE SUPREME MOMENTS OF TRAVEL ARE BORN
OF BEAUTY AND STRANGENESS IN EQUAL PARTS; THE
FIRST PANDERS TO THE SENSES, THE SECOND
TO THE MIND."

Robert Bryant

Waiting for that next travel opportunity can seem like an eternity. Sometimes I begin thinking and planning my next trip halfway through my current trip. This is usually the result of a conversation with other backpackers of places they recently visited or plan to visit. Shared enthusiasm about the places we have visited helps feed the insatiable travel appetite of backpackers.

> "TRAVEL IS AS MUCH A PASSION AS AMBITION OR LOVE"
> *L.E. Landon*

Time and money are the two most essential elements that a traveler must possess. Backpackers understand that reducing the cost of travel allows those with budget concerns to still travel and those without to travel longer. Backpackers are always looking for ways to reduce travel costs. Preparation begins at home before the trip. You should research all aspects of your planned trip from low cost airfare to budget accommodations and food. Bargaining for goods and services becomes second nature to backpackers. It is expected in many countries.

Learning to live with less is an added benefit of backpacking. I now realize that many material things I once considered necessities were really luxuries. Backpackers, in general, are oblivious to the need of accumulating possessions. While most still need jobs that provide shelter, food and transportation, seldom do they purchase that which is unnecessary. A couple from New Zealand could not understand why Americans need to purchase $40,000 automobiles. They see automobiles as a method of transportation rather than a status symbol. While those who work hard have the right to spend their money on any luxuries they want, it just does not correspond with the backpacker mentality. Many Americans begin downsizing, spending less and traveling more as they get older. This would be a great lesson to learn while still young. Some mature backpackers (including myself) have sold everything and begun their pursuit of becoming global nomads.

> "I WOULD RATHER HAVE A LIFETIME OF EXPERIENCES THAN A ROOM FULL OF FURNITURE."
> *Anonymous*

Backpacking is hard work but well worth the effort. The rewards include new experiences, new friends and new adventures. The sacrifices for these experiences are extended periods away from family and friends. At least until you have convinced them that you have not lost your mind and to come with you on your next adventure.

> "CERTAINLY TRAVEL IS MORE THAN THE SEEING OF THE SIGHTS; IT IS A CHANGE THAT GOES ON, DEEP AND PERMANENT, IN THE IDEAS OF LIVING."
>
> *Miriam Beard*

WHAT ARE HOSTELS?

Hostels are the lifeblood and pulse of back-packing. They are essentially discount hotels that provide inexpensive lodging, whether dorm or private rooms, great services, great social atmosphere and usually a convenient location, all of which are tailored for the back-packer. Once upon a time, there was a maximum age limit to stay at the youth hostels but no longer. Mature travelers are quickly learning of the many benefits offered by hostels. It is a common occurrence to see families with children staying in private or dorm rooms at hostels. The general impression from those who have not stayed at a hostel is that they are dirty, inexpensive dorms filled with loud and drunken twenty-somethings. Nothing could be further from the truth. While young backpackers still travel with a party-like enthusiasm, all hostels have quiet times for sleeping. The price of an inexpensive hostel dorm bed does come with a loss of privacy. The occasional snorer (earplugs recommended) and other dorm residents coming in late from partying or getting up early to catch the 5 a.m. bus are some of the inconveniences that you may encounter. However, being able to closely interact with people from all walks of life more than makes up for any inconvenience. Private rooms at the hostel allow for more privacy while still providing all the other benefits. Today, hostels are well-kept, economically priced alternatives to hotels that are frequented not only by young travelers but also by families and mature travelers.

INEXPENSIVE LODGING

Hostels are usually the least expensive sleeping option that will be found within a country, region or city. Hostels can be found in almost every country, including the United States. Dorms are male, female or mixed (co-ed). There is usually a choice, but not always. Most dorms have between four and eight bunk beds in each room. Depending on the hostel, there may be more or less. The bed price corresponds to the number of beds in the dorm. A dorm with 4 beds is more expensive than one with 6 or 8 beds. Be sure to ask for a bed on the bottom if a top bunk is not to your liking. However, there may not be an option. Some smaller dorms may have traditional single beds instead of bunk beds. The dorm rooms are ensuite (bathroom in the room) or there are shared bathrooms. Dorm rooms and private rooms that are ensuite are more expensive than rooms with shared bathrooms. The shared bathrooms include separate facilities for men and women. Private rooms in the hostel may be as inexpensive as a dorm bed when shared by one or more fellow travelers and give you the privacy that the dorms do not allow. It will also allow you time to get acquainted with the hostel lifestyle before venturing into a dorm. The price ranges of hostels can be as varied as those of hotels are and depend on the quality of accommodations offered, services provided, location within the town and country you are visiting. I have paid as little as $1.50 a night for a dorm bed in China and as much as $48.00 a night for a dorm bed in Norway. If staying in a hostel for an extended period (week or longer), see if you can negotiate a reduced rate.

SERVICES AND FACILITIES

The services and facilities provided by most hostels are essential to backpackers. Most hostels include free Wi-Fi, internet, a community kitchen, television rooms with DVD's, lounge area, linen, laundry service, lockers and luggage storage, travel information centers and discount tours. Many hostels also offer 24 hour reception and security, swimming pools, restaurant, bar and free breakfast.

The internet is crucial to making travel reservations, researching destinations and keeping connected to home. The community kitchen allows you to buy inexpensive food at the market and prepare meals at the hostel rather than eating out. Everyone writes their name on their food and places it in the refrigerator or pantry. This took a while to get used to but everyone respects the system. The television and lounge areas give you a chance to catch up on the latest news, watch movies and sports, read a book, or interact with other travelers. The laundry service is necessary on occasion when washing your clothes in the sink just is not getting it anymore. Lockers in the dorm rooms give you the freedom to travel around town without having to take everything with you. You should always carry a small padlock in your backpack for the hostel lockers. Luggage storage is another benefit that many hostels offer where you can leave your luggage before checking in and after checking out. The hostel is a great source of information for transportation, restaurants, sights and discount tours. Most hostels have copies of the bus transportation schedules including their departure times, which is very convenient for planning the next leg of your journey. Many hostels can also help you buy tickets for the train or bus to your next destination, which is very helpful if you do not speak the language. Discount tours at hostels are usually the lowest available, primarily because everyone staying at the hostel is cost conscious. In many cases, shuttle service is available from the hostel to your next destination.

24-hour reception is important if coming into the city on a late bus, train or plane. The best hostels have very good security and knowing that undesirables do not have access to the hostel makes it much easier to sleep. Hostels that have a curfew lock their doors at night and others require all backpackers to leave for a few hours each day (lockout), to clean the hostel. Swimming pools are always a nice benefit especially after a long day of hiking and seeing the sights. Many hostels also have a restaurant and/or bar which provides inexpensive meals and drinks that are cost-friendly for the backpacker. Free breakfast is a staple in many hostels and when offered consists of toast, jam, cereal, fruit, coffee and juice. Cheese, ham and bread are also included in South America. These additions provide a wonderful opportunity to make a couple of sandwiches for lunch. While not the most exciting breakfast, it is FREE, a word that quickly gets the attention of most backpackers.

SOCIAL ATMOSPHERE

The social atmosphere is what I consider the best asset of the hostel, especially for the solo traveler. The need to share your travel experiences can be overwhelming at times. The opportunity to speak to other travelers is almost constant; whether in a dorm, the lounge area, community kitchen or hostel bar. "What country are you from?" followed by "How long are you traveling?" and "Where are you going?" seem to always be the first questions asked by backpackers. We, as a group, are inquisitive by nature and interested in obtaining as much travel information as possible. When just arriving at a new destination, travelers that have been there for several days can provide valuable information. Everyone always seems to have a list of things to do and not do for the area. It is your job to provide this same information to new arrivals after you have been there for a few days. Sitting around the lounge area sharing travel stories and advice is great fun and may provide information for another trip. Listening to someone speak about traveling in a country that you have not yet visited always gives a personal perspective that you cannot get in a guidebook. Hostels provide an excellent opportunity to make new friends and possibly travel companions. Backpackers are always looking for a way to share expenses.

CONVENIENT LOCATION

Hostels are usually located in a convenient location. Most are near major transportation hubs, such as a bus or train station, near the town centre or near the major tourist attractions. In many situations, you are close enough to walk from the bus or train station. Also, they are usually located near many restaurants and nightlife. The location is usually one of the deciding factors when I choose a hostel. Hostelworld gives backpacker ratings for location for each hostel it lists on its website.

FINDING A HOSTEL

Finding a hostel is easy with a little help from the internet. There are many websites that provide hostel bookings such as hostelworld. com, hihostels.com, hostels.com, and hostelbookers.com, just to name a few. These websites provide prices, availability, ratings, reviews, and facilities offered, which can be very helpful in deciding on a hostel. Some websites may charge a booking fee or membership fee, so be sure to look for those and see what benefits each offers. Hostelling International (HI) sells a discount card that gives 10% off its many hostels and other services around the world. Hostelworld.com is probably the best known and most widely used but I suggest that you try several when searching for a hostel. The hostel itself may even have a website that charges less for the accommodation. Not all websites carry the same listings. Many independent hostels are not linked to any website, other than their own, mainly due to the fact they do not want to pay the fee associated with the listing. Often, I will use Google or Yahoo Search to search for listings of other hostels at my destination. You should check out several of these websites to familiarize yourself with them.

Travel guides also provide a list of hostels that they have visited and consider the best available at the time of publication according to price. One problem with hostels highlighted in travel guides is they tend to be a bit overcrowded, due to the added publicity. Be sure to check the websites for availability before going to one of these and to ensure they are still open.

My Initial Hostel Experience

I was fifty-one years old when I went to Europe for two months on my first backpacking trip. Since I was traveling solo, I knew that I would have to stay in hostels to afford this trip. However, my inexperience and fear of staying in a hostel dorm caused me to book private rooms at the hostel. While still much cheaper than any other accommodations available, the cost was two to three times more expensive than a dorm bed. My bank account suffered greatly and after that trip, I was determined to try hostel dorms on my next trip. I have stayed in many dorms since that first trip to Europe in 2006 and most have been pleasant and rewarding experiences. It is now my favorite type of accommodation, mostly due to the close interaction with other backpackers. I stay in a dorm the majority of the time but when I feel a need for privacy, I book a private room. Sometimes you just want to be alone. My biggest fear on staying in a dorm was being much older than the majority of the other dorm occupants. I soon realized that no one saw me as older, just another backpacker.

Trevi Fountain in Rome, Italy

Florence, Italy

CHAPTER 3

WHY TRAVEL?

> "THE WORLD IS A BOOK AND THOSE WHO DO
> NOT TRAVEL ONLY READ ONE PAGE."
> *Saint Augustine*

Most in the United States travel for business or vacation. Until recently, less than 20% of all U.S. citizens had a passport. The majority of foreign travelers (most of whom get passports at birth) believe that number is so low due to the large variety of destinations within the States. While partially true, I believe the real reason is our fear of unfamiliar countries, foods, language, currency, customs and

culture. We prefer to travel in our own comfort zone, which is within our own country
and sometimes within our own state or region. Our trips are usually for vacation rather than travel. Vacation means escape while
travel is more about learning, experiences
and adventure.

"WE TRAVEL, INITIALLY, TO LOSE OURSELVES;
AND WE TRAVEL, NEXT, TO FIND OURSELVES. WE
TRAVEL TO OPEN OUR HEARTS AND EYES AND
LEARN MORE ABOUT THE WORLD THAN OUR
NEWSPAPERS WILL ACCOMMODATE. WE TRAVEL TO
BRING WHAT LITTLE WE CAN, IN OUR IGNORANCE
AND KNOWLEDGE, TO THOSE PARTS OF THE GLOBE
WHOSE RICHES ARE DIFFERENTLY DISPERSED. AND
WE TRAVEL, IN ESSENCE, TO BECOME YOUNG FOOLS
AGAIN- TO SLOW TIME DOWN AND GET TAKEN IN,
AND FALL IN LOVE ONCE MORE."

Pico Iyer

The backpacker seeks out the differences in
other countries and cultures and embraces
them. This is done in the pursuit of education, exploration and self-discovery.

EDUCATION

"DON'T TELL ME HOW EDUCATED YOU ARE, TELL
ME HOW MUCH YOU HAVE TRAVELED."
Mohammed

The education aspect of traveling includes finding out that people around the world are similar even though they may have different beliefs. While the language, religion, culture and customs may seem strange to us, people all over the world rear families, spend time with their friends, go to work and worship in the religion of their choice. Travel can also teach you how it feels to be a minority. While standing in an enormous, crowded train station in Beijing, China, I realized that I was the outsider. While trying to figure out how to buy a ticket, several Chinese college students approached me and asked if they could practice their English. I took this opportunity to enlist their help in purchasing my ticket. They asked questions about the United States and I asked questions about China. It was amazing to see what misconceptions we both had about each other's countries.

The students could be mistaken for those at any college in the United States. They were dressed in jeans, backpacks and t-shirts and constantly texting on their phones. Until you have traveled to another country and met its people, you have to rely upon other people's opinions and observations.

> "THE USE OF TRAVELING IS TO REGULATE IMAGINATION BY REALITY, AND INSTEAD OF THINKING HOW THINGS MAY BE, TO SEE THEM AS THEY REALLY ARE."
>
> *Samuel Jackson*

I will never forget sharing a taxi with two Chinese college students who asked me where I was from. When I told them Louisiana, they both looked at me in absolute shock. They spoke a few words in Chinese to each other while staring at me. I asked them if there was a problem and they said that they were just surprised that I was not black since I lived in Louisiana. They were of the impression that only African Americans lived in Louisiana. They said their only knowledge of Louisiana was news videos they had seen during Hurricane Katrina and that everyone in those videos was black. This illustrates how media and our lack of personal knowledge can give us a false impression of a country. Possibly the best chance for peace in this world is for us to realize and embrace our similarities rather than focusing on our differences. All friendships begin by noticing the similarities. Travel gives us this opportunity. On many occasions, I have been the first American that those from other countries have met. Your responsibility as a traveler is to represent your country well and respect the people, their customs and culture of the country you are visiting. It is a privilege to visit their country, not a right. The foundation the United States was built upon was the right to be different. We should afford those same rights to others while traveling.

> "TRAVEL IS FATAL TO PREJUDICE, BIGOTRY AND NARROW-MINDEDNESS."
>
> *Mark Twain*

Pandas in Chengu, China

EXPLORATION

Exploration and adventure are also great reasons to travel. Seeing and experiencing new sights, people and places seem to regenerate that "childish enthusiasm" and "youthful exuberance".

> "WITHOUT NEW EXPERIENCES, SOMETHING INSIDE OF US SLEEPS. THE SLEEPER MUST AWAKEN."
> *Frank Herbert*

Forgetful of my age, I have been skydiving out of a helicopter in Switzerland, bungee jumping in New Zealand, hiking in the Himalayas and scuba diving on the Great

Barrier Reef. My own personal "bucket list" has been shredded and rewritten many times. Whether whitewater rafting down the Grand Canyon or taking the slow boat up the Amazon, your adventure awaits. There is nothing like an adrenaline rush to make one feel alive. While your exploration or adventure does not have to be "death defying", it is important that you step out of your comfort zone.

> "TWENTY YEARS FROM NOW YOU WILL BE MORE DISAPPOINTED BY THE THINGS YOU DIDN'T DO THAN BY THE ONES YOU DID DO. SO THROW OFF THE BOWLINES, SAIL AWAY FROM THE SAFE HARBOR. CATCH THE TRADE WINDS IN YOUR SAILS. EXPLORE. DREAM. DISCOVER."
>
> *Mark Twain*

Backpacking around The World

Whitewater rafting in the Grand Canyon

Slow boat down the Amazon River

Piranha breakfast I caught in the Amazon

SELF-DISCOVERY

> **"I SOON REALIZED THAT NO JOURNEY CARRIES ONE FAR UNLESS, AS IT EXTENDS INTO THE WORLD AROUND US, IT GOES AN EQUAL DISTANCE INTO THE WORLD WITHIN."**
>
> *Lillian Smith*

Self-discovery and the ongoing pursuit for purpose occupy much of our life. Traveling gives you the opportunity to redefine, re-invent and rediscover yourself. Sometimes we are just looking for a new direction; and traveling to a new country with new sights, new ideas and new people may be just the thing to give us that insight. There are many life-changing opportunities around the world. For me, it was climbing Kilimanjaro and going on safari in Tanzania. Standing on the summit of Africa's highest mountain (19,340 feet) at sunrise will always be one of my greatest journeys. Adding a four-day safari to the Serengeti and Ngorongor Crater to see the incredible wildlife of Africa up close made this trip almost too good to be true.

Mount Kilimanjaro, Tanzania

Serengeti, Tanzania

Lion stalking wildebeest on Serengeti

The best time to start your adventure is today. For you, it may be touring the wine country in Tuscany, walking on the Great Wall of China or a cruise to Antarctica. With so much diversity and budget options around the world, finding travel destinations to your liking will not be a problem.

> "HAVE WE NOT STOOD HERE LIKE TREES IN THE GROUND LONG ENOUGH?"
> *Walt Whitman*

Backpacking gives you the opportunity to do many of these instead of selecting just one by traveling cheaper. Once you make that "life-changing" trip, maybe you will gain a completely new perspective on life and its purpose. Now is the time to stop dreaming and make it a reality?

> "FIND OUT WHO YOU ARE AND DO IT ON PURPOSE."
> *Dolly Parton*

Great Wall of China

Antarctica

TRAVELING SOLO OR WITH SOMEONE?

Whether you decide to travel solo, with friends, with a partner or with family, each situation has its own advantages and disadvantages that greatly affect how you travel and what you can do.

SOLO

The biggest advantage in traveling solo is your total freedom when making travel plans. The biggest disadvantage is lack of companionship. For me, traveling solo was my only option when I first started backpacking.

I was unable to find anyone willing or that had the time to go on a backpacking adventure. I had talked about traveling to Europe for over 30 years but there always seemed to be a reason not to go. I finally realized that if I wanted to travel, I would have to take things into my own hands and head out for faraway lands by myself.

> "THE MAN WHO GOES OUT ALONE CAN START TODAY, BUT HE WHO TRAVELS WITH ANOTHER MUST WAIT TILL THAT OTHER IS READY."
> *Henry David Thoreau*

Neuschwanstein Castle in Germany

Salzburg, Austria

I believe that traveling solo was how back-packing was intended. By definition, it is supposed to be "independent" travel. You should always consider yourself traveling solo even in the company of others. When traveling by yourself you are completely free to pursue the dreams and goals that you hoped to achieve without worrying about a fellow traveler's wishes. The major advantage is you are able to travel without having to consult anyone before making your decisions. You can eat at whatever restaurant you like, do the activities that you like and change your travel plans and destinations at a moments notice without someone else having to agree. There is something exciting about traveling to a foreign country without a traveling companion to act as a safety net. You have to rely on yourself for every decision along the trip. After backpacking solo, you are assured of returning with greater self-confidence. I believe the best reason for traveling solo is that you just want to be by yourself and everything that reminds you of home. What better way to gain a new perspective on life than separating yourself from everything that constitutes your life, as you know it.

The biggest disadvantage is lack of familiar companionship and being unable to share your travel experiences with someone you know. Trying to explain the places and sights that you have seen never fully translates to those who have not been there. However, backpackers are a very close group and traveling solo will not be as lonely as you might think. Each country has its favorite backpacker hostels, restaurants and bars where it is easy to meet fellow travelers and share experiences. Meeting new people from diverse backgrounds is an educational experience in itself. Sharing a meal and drinks with new backpacker-friends from other countries is a great way to expand your global knowledge. Solo women travelers may have additional safety concerns and should take additional precautions while traveling. Meeting and traveling with new friends is almost a way of life in the backpacking world. Regardless of where you travel, you will most likely run into some of the same backpackers throughout your trip. It is also possible to travel solo with friends, family or a partner by allowing them to share a portion of your trip in which they have an interest. This gives you the best of both worlds.

I suggest for those who are a little unsure about backpacking solo for the first time, to make Costa Rica their first destination. Everyone speaks English, transportation is simple and accommodations are above average and easy to find. I met a young college student from Texas in 2008 who was on his first backpacking trip and admitted to being a little nervous about the experience. I asked why he chose Costa Rica for his first solo adventure out of the country. He said, "Costa Rica is like backpacking with training wheels." It is so true.

FRIENDS

Traveling with friends is a little more complicated. You must first find a friend who wants to travel rather than go on vacation. You should make sure they understand you are traveling on a budget so that accommodation choices will not become a problem while on the trip. They must also want to see the same countries, the same sights and travel for the same length of time. Finally, you must decide whether spending 24 hours a day for the next few weeks or months is an option that you can live with. Someone whose disposition and moods are different from you might wear on your nerves over several weeks. Even the best of friends have some things that irritate each other. You must weigh all these factors with the advantages of being able to share private rooms in hostels, share travel expenses and having a friend to share all the wonderful experiences. A traveling companion also comes in handy if you get sick or need a little emotional support. If you are unsure about traveling with a friend for an extended period, you should try a shorter trip first. My brother, Morgan, traveled through Europe over a summer with fellow law students. They would travel together as long as they wanted, then go their separate ways and meet back up later. This is a great idea for friends who are traveling together but want to see separate sights. Split apart and meet up later.

Venice, Italy

Cliffs of Mohr, Ireland

Windmills in the Netherlands

WITH A PARTNER

Traveling with a partner may have the most rewards and presents the most danger. Backpacking can be a wonderful way to get to know each other regardless of whether you have been together for a long time or not. Spending a lot of time together in close quarters can tell you a lot about a person. It can also point out flaws that maybe you did not see because each was able to maintain a certain level of privacy. The major advantage of backpacking as a couple is being able to share those special moments that will bring you closer.

It is important while traveling with a partner not to spend every moment together. Shopping and walking around on your own gives both parties some privacy and the opportunity to explore on their own. Traveling at a leisurely pace is more enjoyable and keeps things from getting too stressful. It is also important to treat yourselves when backpacking. Eating at a nice restaurant or staying at a nice hotel can be a welcome respite from budget travel after you or your "significant other" has been through a particularly stressful time. Sometimes you have to take a vacation within your backpacking trip.

FAMILY

- -

Traveling with family is the one mode of travel that I enjoy most. While traveling with my family is only part of my solo journey, it gives me the opportunity to share backpacking with my family, especially the grandchildren. I recently was able to travel with my oldest son, daughter-in-law and two grandchildren to Costa Rica for 10 days. They had become interested in my travels with the help of my travel blogs and were ready to give backpacking a try. They were rewarded with volcanoes, white-water rafting, zip lining through the cloud forest, monkeys and beautiful beaches. Backpacking with family will always have restrictions of what sights they are interested in seeing and how long they can travel. Family travel for a portion of your trip is a great way to share travel experiences with people you love. Teaching your family to backpack and see the world will be one of the greatest gifts that you can give them. As a bonus, grandchildren love to visit the grandparents when they are traveling around the world. Giving a family member their first passport as a Christmas or birthday present will be something they will never forget and which will change their life.

"TRAVELING IN THE COMPANY OF THOSE WE LOVE IS HOME IN MOTION."

Leigh Hunt

TRAVEL GUIDES
(THE BACKPACKER'S
ENCYCLOPEDIA)

A travel guide may be the most important item that you will purchase before your backpacking trip. It gives you great information on planning the trip, traveling through the region and returning home. The travel guide provides comprehensive information on getting started, the country's highlights, sample itineraries, transportation, sleeping and eating, health and language. Also included are maps of the country, regions and cities. Anything not included above can be located in the country's directory in the back of the travel guide.

Lonely Planet, Rough Guide, Frommer's, Fodor's and Rick Steve's are just a few examples of popular travel guides. Each is different and you should look through several at the bookstore to see which fits you the best. Buying online may save you some money after you have found one that you like. Local libraries also have copies of travel guides, though they may not be the latest editions. Lonely Planet offers individual sections of their travel guides, which can be purchased online at reduced prices. When buying a travel guide make sure to get the latest edition available. You do not want to search for a restaurant or hostel that is featured in the guide but no longer in business.

GETTING STARTED

Getting started includes when to go, costs and money. When to go provides information on weather, peak tourist and shoulder seasons and festivals. Traveling during shoulder season (before or after the peak tourist season) will be less expensive and less crowded. Cost gives you an idea of how much money it takes to backpack through a country including accommodation, transportation and food while traveling on a shoestring budget. This gives you a good idea of the absolute minimum you would need to travel when added to the airfare needed to reach your destination. In addition, there is usually a daily budget estimate for mid-range and high-end travelers.

Money explains the country's currency and gives you the exchange rate at the time of publication. A current currency exchange rate can be found online before traveling. Travel guides advise of the availability of ATMs and whether travelers' checks are accepted.

HIGHLIGHTS

The country's highlights include the best tourist sights and activities for each region or town. Examples include best activities, beaches, festivals and events, historic sites, parks and natural attractions and wildlife.

SAMPLE ITINERARIES

Travel guides also provide sample itineraries for periods of seven days, two weeks, one month or several months. These itineraries provide the best route to travel based on your interests. These are especially helpful when traveling through several countries. Having a prospective itinerary allows you to plan transportation and accommodations in advance. It also gives you a period in which to purchase your airline tickets for your departure and return.

TRANSPORTATION

Transportation includes getting there and away and getting around. Getting there and away lists all forms of transportation that go to and leave your intended destination. These include air, boat, bus and train. Prices are quoted for some of the most popular routes but are only accurate as of the date of publication. Getting around usually includes the best way to get around town and its costs.

SLEEPING AND EATING

The sleeping and eating sections are reviewed personally by the travel guide's staff and considered the best based on costs and quality of accommodations available. The majority are budget based but there are always a few mid-range options listed. The eating section provides a list of inexpensive restaurants with a variety of food. The reviews include addresses, phone numbers, websites, price range and overall opinion of each specific location.

HEALTH

The health section provides a list of required and/or recommended vaccinations, a medical checklist and infectious diseases, if any, listed for that region.

LANGUAGE

One of the most useful sections is that on language. It provides pronunciation and useful travel phrases. While most tourist destinations speak at least some English, it is always nice to know and try to speak some of the country's language. Learning how to say or read "toilet" in the country's language always seems to come in handy.

MAPS

There are many maps of the country, region and towns, which provide assistance in locating accommodations, restaurants, bus stations and tourist sights. Additionally, they are helpful in planning your next route and destination.

COUNTRY DIRECTORY

The country's directory includes general information on accommodations, climate, customs, dangers & annoyances, internet access, toilets, visas and documents, women travelers, volunteering and working.

INSTANT TRAVEL INFORMATION

When a backpacker is in need of information, pulling out his or her travel guide is usually everyone's first choice. Travel guides are compact and give the backpacker more information than any other source. It is a rare occasion when you do not see someone perusing through a travel guide while sitting at the hostel. Do not bring two or three different travel guides in an effort to have a variety of information. That is simply over-kill and while not too heavy in beginning, will quickly become so. Remember that the travel guide should be used as a "guide" and current research and discovery on your own are a large part of the excitement of independent travel.

WHERE, WHEN AND HOW LONG TO TRAVEL

Where, when and for how long to travel are all intertwined for the budget backpacker, especially if budget and time constraints are an issue. Deciding to travel is always the hardest decision. However, realizing that you cannot see it all in one trip is the most important thing to realize when deciding where, when and for how long.

WHERE TO TRAVEL

Making a list of "where to travel" is always the first step. You should look to your dreams, friends and family, travel television programs, magazines, tour companies, travel agents and travel guides when searching for potential travel destinations. Budget may also be a determining factor.

I believe that "dreams" should be at the forefront when making your list. As we grow up and get older, we all have memories of places and countries that we had hoped to visit "someday". Now is the perfect time to take it off your "someday" list and place it on your "today" list. Maybe it is time to make your dream a reality.

Friends and family are great resources for developing your list of places to travel. They can give you firsthand knowledge of travel destinations they have visited. They will also know if it is somewhere that you might enjoy. Also, friends and family travel photos are much more enjoyable if there is a possibility that you may be traveling there.

The Travel Channel is one of my favorite television channels. It gives the opportunity to see new and exotic countries that I have not visited and maybe not even considered before as a travel destination. The hosts are usually accompanied by a local who gives highlights and insights to his country. While some of the material is commercially driven, there is still an opportunity to see the beautiful sights and learn more about the locals. Television provides a much better viewpoint of a country than one can get through the pictures of a brochure or travel guide.

Travel magazines are an excellent source for finding places that you would like to visit. I really enjoy Arthur Frommer's *Budget Travel* and *Traveler* from National Geographic. Both have inexpensive subscriptions and provide information on every aspect of travel, especially discount travel. Travel tips are provided in every issue and there is a free travel information directory in the back of the magazines. Since it is free, I order anything and everything that seems interesting. Upon receiving the information, I place all the information in a specific country or region folder for future reference. I mark each folder with the best times to visit and this becomes my own personal travel library.

Tour companies such as Gate 1, Intrepid, Adventure Life and Wilderness Travel, to name a few, provide excellent information on travel opportunities and provide great itineraries based on years of experience. I order every free brochure from every travel company to find out what each country has to offer. I cut out all the itineraries, place them in my travel library and use them as a guide in my own independent travel.

Travel agents can provide a wide variety of information on favorite destinations. This includes travel brochures that can give you an idea of what each country has to offer. While most tours offered at travel agencies are too expensive for backpackers, this does not stop one from assembling as much travel information as possible.

Travel guides provide the most information regarding a country or region as previously outlined. They also include many color photographs depicting the highlights, activities and scenery of each country. Looking through travel guides in a bookstore or local library is a great way to introduce you to new countries.

Budget may also be an important factor in deciding where to travel. If you are on a tight budget, then you must eliminate all countries that have high travel costs such as Europe, unless you are planning a short trip. Europe is much more expensive than traveling in Asia, Central or South America. Travel guides provide a daily travel budget estimate for each country, which is a very useful planning tool. Even some countries within a region are less expensive to travel than other countries. For example, Costa Rica is almost twice as expensive as traveling in Nicaragua and Western Europe is more expensive than Eastern Europe.

> "SOME PARTS OF THE WORLD YOU MAKE A CONSCIOUS EFFORT TO VISIT AND OTHERS HAVE TO WAIT UNTIL FATE DELIVERS YOU THERE."
> *Tony Hawks*

Sukhotai, Thailand

Woman shucking corn in Nepal

WHEN TO TRAVEL

Once you have created a list of potential travel destinations, you have to decide "when to travel". This is usually based upon when you are available to travel, climate of countries you wish to visit and your budget.

Hopefully you have great flexibility for when you can travel. If not, you will have to match the time for which you can travel to your list of potential destinations and the best time to travel there. Keeping a travel library and marking each country or region with the best times to visit will be very helpful in deciding when to travel. Travel guides provide the best and worst times to travel within a country or region.

The climate of some countries varies greatly depending on the time of the year and it is very important when deciding the best time to visit your destination. Travel guides give climate information for each country or region and advise you when is the best time to travel in that country or region based on the activities that you plan on pursuing. You most likely would not want to hike in the Himalayas in the winter, nor endure a sweltering summer in Australia. Also, the seasons are opposite in the southern hemisphere, so be careful not to plan a trip to New Zealand in our summer unless you plan on snow skiing. Many countries have specific monsoon and hurricane seasons that you may want to avoid. The best weather is usually the peak tourist season but the shoulder season (before and after the peak season) can also have great weather and fewer crowds in most instances. In addition, if the travel guides say that, a certain time is the "rainy season"; this does not mean it rains constantly every day. In many cases, it may rain less than an hour each day on average. Sometimes this can provide a welcome relief to the heat while traveling along regions close to the equator.

Budget is the final piece of the puzzle of "when to travel". Traveling during the shoulder season (before and after peak season) is always less expensive and less crowded. This makes accommodations cheaper and easier to find. Many hostel dorms may be empty or only have a few travelers, which is always nice. I have been alone in a dorm with seven empty beds on more than one occasion while traveling in the shoulder season. In addition, when accommodations are not full there is room for bargaining. The exchange rate of the dollar to other countries' currency should also be watched. If a foreign country has recently devalued the U.S. currency, it may be best to wait and visit when the U.S. Dollar is stronger. For me, airline prices dictate where I travel. Airline tickets are usually a major expenditure and I am always looking for that "special" airline price to one of the destinations on my list. To get a great deal you must be ready to purchase your ticket at a moments notice.

HOW LONG TO TRAVEL

The length of your trip is usually decided by the amount of time you have to travel, the countries that you would like to visit and your budget. Traveling slowly helps you travel inexpensively and allows you to travel for longer periods.

> "ONE DOES NOT DISCOVER NEW LANDS WITHOUT CONSENTING TO LOSE SIGHT OF THE SHORE FOR A VERY LONG TIME."
>
> *Andre Gide*

Sample itineraries, found in guidebooks, on websites and in travel brochures are a great planning tool when trying to decide which countries to visit and what to see in a specific period.

The maximum time that you can travel may be affected by many factors such as job, family or previous commitments. The more time you have available, the more options you have. The first step is determining exactly how long you can travel and you must plan everything else within that period.

Next, determine the countries that you want to visit and the things you would like to do while in those countries. Difficulty in getting to your destination and getting back home must also be considered. If possible, plan your trip by arriving in one destination and flying back home from another destination. This is known as an open-jaw flight. It keeps the traveler from backtracking and saves time and money. Careful planning and researching sample itineraries can give you an idea of the amount of time needed to accomplish everything you would like to do on this trip. The sample itineraries provide the most efficient route to see and do everything you have planned. Travel guides provide itineraries that are time specific such as 1 week, 2 weeks, 1 month or several months. Each lists the day-to-day destinations along with their highlights. Websites such as intrepidtravel.com and gate1travel.com are another good source for sample itineraries. In addition, catalogs from tour companies have sample itineraries for each country or region. I always cut these out and save them in my travel library (folders with info on countries I have collected) for future reference. You can combine, alter, add or delete portions of any of these itineraries to make your own that suits your specific interests. After making these adjustments and making a final itinerary, you will have a great idea of how long it will take for the trip. Making the final itinerary only means that you have a road map with a beginning and ending destination over a specific time. A backpacker's itinerary is never etched in stone and is constantly being revised based on new knowledge and interests.

> "THE TRAIL IS THE THING, NOT THE END OF THE TRAIL. TRAVEL TOO FAST AND YOU WILL MISS ALL THAT YOU ARE TRAVELING FOR."
> *Louis L'Amour*

Simple Version

Make a list of several travel destinations whose climate conditions are favorable when you have the time to travel and are within your budget. Prepare itineraries for these trips and watch for low airline fares on the internet. Since you know when you can travel and for how long you will be traveling, the airline ticket is the only missing piece. If an incredible price to one of your destinations appears, buy the ticket and go.

"Journeys, like artists, are born and not made. A thousand differing circumstances contribute to them, few of them willed or determined by the will."

Lawrence Durrell

Passports And Visas

Before traveling, you must make sure you have a valid passport and any visas that are necessary for the country or countries that you plan on visiting. A passport is an official document that certifies one's identity and citizenship and permits a citizen to travel abroad. A visa is an official authorization appended to a passport, permitting entry into and travel within a particular country or region.

Passport

Before traveling you must make sure that you have a valid passport with enough vacant pages for visas for the countries you expect to visit. Some countries require that your passport be valid for at least six (6) months or longer beyond the date of your trip. If you do not have a valid passport, make sure to apply early enough to receive it before your trip date. In most cases, you can apply at a regional office for an expedited passport if you can prove you are under time constraints. The U.S. Department of State provides information at http://travel.state.gov/passport on renewing or applying for a passport. Make copies of your passport and keep them separate in case it is lost or stolen. You should also leave a copy of your passport with family or friends. This will make getting a new passport at the U.S. Embassy much easier and quicker. Some people scan their passport and other important information on a memory stick to keep in case of emergency. Be sure and carry your passport in a safe location, preferably a money belt. Passports are a valuable commodity in foreign countries and are frequently the target of thieves.

VISAS

Visa requirements vary from country to country. While travel guides provide visa information on every country, the information is only as good as its publication date. A quick search on the internet can give you current visa requirements. The U.S. Department of State provides this information at www. travel.state.gov/visa. In most countries, you can easily obtain a visa at the border for a nominal fee or no fee at all. However, some countries such as China and Brazil require that you obtain a visa from their embassy before you travel and the cost is approximately $150 U.S. dollars for each. Visas are issued for different times ranging from 24 hours in Myanmar to a period of 10 years in Brazil (though only valid for 180 days per year). You must exit the country before your visa expires or face daily fines. Some tour companies offer "visa runs" which transport you to the border for you to exit and then immediately re-enter the country and return to your original destination. This restarts the time for you to remain in the country. You may get additional pages for your passport while traveling at the U.S. Embassy if there are not enough pages for the countries that you plan to visit. You should also keep extra passport pictures with you, as some countries require a passport photo with the visa application.

Some countries also require that you have an onward ticket, which can be a train or bus ticket to another country. Your return airline ticket is also considered an onward ticket. Be careful at border checkpoints and only pay money to border officials. It can be confusing at times while trying to get a visa at the border and there are those who try to take advantage of unsuspecting tourists. Border officials and licensed currency converters should have an official badge.

"THE TRAVELER MUST BE BORN AGAIN IN THE ROAD AND EARN A PASSPORT FROM THE ELEMENTS."
Henry David Thoreau

Bill Passman

Karst Formations on Li River

Iguazu Falls, Brazil

73

PLANNING THE TRIP

After deciding where, when and how long you will travel, you are ready to purchase your airline tickets. After purchasing your tickets, you must book your initial sleeping accommodations and any additional local transportation that may be necessary. Then you must make a final estimate of your trip cost and take care of all money matters necessary for your trip. An additional consideration is whether to purchase travel insurance or not.

INTERNATIONAL AIRFARE

Finding the best flight for the lowest cost and the fewest plane changes is one of the most important tasks in planning the trip. The lowest price may involve many plane changes before arriving at your final destination. This is another reason we pack light and only use carry-on luggage. The cost of airline tickets is a major expense in most trips. I always have at least two destinations and two itineraries prepared for almost every time of the year. That way, when an unbelievable airfare appears on the internet I am prepared to purchase the ticket before they are sold out. To get low fares you must be prepared to buy your ticket at a moments notice. Once I was considering a trip to Costa Rica when a roundtrip flight from Miami to Lima, Peru came across the internet for only $198.00 including fuel surcharges and taxes. I quickly looked for a roundtrip flight from New Orleans (my home airport) to Miami and found one for $110.00. I checked the best times to travel and itineraries in my Peru travel folder (from my Travel Library) and booked the flights within 15 minutes. Once I had the airline tickets, I began to plan the rest of my trip.

Finding inexpensive airline fares has become much easier due to the number of airline search engines available. Some of my favorites are kayak.com, expedia.com, mobissimo.com, orbitz.com, cheaptickets.

com and travelocity.com. Other popular sites include momondo.com and dohop.com. A great discount airline to Central America, Colombia and the Caribbean is Spirit Airlines (spiritair.com) whose hub is in Ft. Lauderdale, Florida. Airfarewatchdog.com is the site that I use the most to find national and international airfare specials. Their site allows you to pick several departure cities and they email you airfare specials several times weekly. I especially like sites that have options for flexible dates. This allows the site to search up to 3 days before and 3 days after your proposed date to search for cheaper flights. You should also be aware that flights on Tuesday, Wednesday and Saturday are historically less expensive than the other days of the week. Also, some of the least expensive days to travel are holidays, especially Thanksgiving, Christmas Eve or Christmas day. The best days to search for low fares are usually late Monday or early Tuesday. Finding inexpensive airfare is like putting a puzzle together, with destinations, travel dates and prices being the puzzle pieces.

Another decision you must make is whether to fly open-jaw or not. Open-jaw means flying into one destination and returning home from another. This keeps the traveler

from having to backtrack to get to your original destination for the return flight. On my
trip to Asia in 2008, I bought an open-jaw
ticket with Beijing as my original destination and Hong Kong as my departure destination. The price was the same as if I had
flown roundtrip to Beijing. By purchasing
the open-jaw ticket, I was able to travel by
land throughout China, Laos, Cambodia,
Malaysia and Thailand before taking the
short flight from Bangkok to Hong Kong.
The flight from Bangkok to Hong Kong was
only $130 whereas Bangkok to Beijing would
have cost me $650. This may not work ev-
ery time but is something to consider when
planning a trip. You must weigh the extra
cost, if any, compared to the cost and time
of getting back to your original destination.

Boy fishing on Mekong River

It is well known in travel circles that buying two airline tickets instead of one can sometimes save you a lot of money. Gateway cities usually have the best prices for international destinations. For example, New York and Newark usually have the best prices for Europe, Miami and Ft. Lauderdale typically have the best prices for the Caribbean, Central and South America and Los Angeles for flights to New Zealand, Australia and Asia. It may be cheaper to buy a ticket from your home to the gateway city and then to your final destination. This also allows you to visit the gateway city for a few days if you have the time and plan it properly.

When searching for airfares for two people, be sure to check the price for one traveler. Sometimes the best rates are for one person. If so, just buy two single tickets.

If you find a flight and price that you like on a particular search engine, it cannot hurt to try a few other search engines and even go directly to that airlines website to check prices before purchasing.

When looking for inexpensive airline tickets, make sure that all fuel surcharges and taxes are included in the listed price. I cannot tell you how many times I thought I had found an incredible deal only to find out that the "extra charges" were as much as the price quoted. Most search engines include all charges but double check.

Many airline search engines and airline websites request that you enter a passport number for an international flight. Most do not require that you fill in this information but some airlines do. If waiting on your passport and you are unable to book without a passport number, call the airline directly. A better idea is to make sure you have obtained a passport before planning any trips.

Allow time for delay when booking connecting flights. You do not want to miss a connecting flight due to a delay in arrival. In addition, terminals are so large it may take a while to get from one gate to another.

Choose your specific seat on the plane as soon as it is possible. Window seats have a view, are a little more comfortable if you plan to sleep and people getting up during the flight do not bother you. On the other hand, aisle seats have more legroom (in the aisle) and allow you to get up without disturbing others on your row. If traveling as a twosome, select a window seat and an aisle seat, leaving the middle seat empty. If the flight is not full, you will most likely have the entire row to yourselves. However, if the flight is full, most likely the person in the middle would be willing to switch for an aisle or window seat. Do not forget to walk around the plane and stretch your legs, especially on long flights.

If you are delayed at the airport and your flight is cancelled or severely delayed, use your cell phone to reschedule or get wait listed rather than wait in a long line. You are more likely to get accurate information about departure times and other flights. Be sure to program your airline reservation number in your phone before you go.

SLEEPING

- -

The most important accommodation booking is the first night of your trip. This should be booked and confirmed before your trip begins. Websites such as hostelworld.com, hi-hostels.com, hostels.com and hostelbookers.com will provide you with ratings, reviews, price, availability and any other information needed to find a hostel, family guesthouse or budget hotel. The website will do all the booking and send you a confirmation that also provides directions for getting to the accommodation upon arrival from the bus station, train station or airport. Since this may be your first experience in the country, make sure the accommodation meets all your requirements such as safety, comfort level and location. Meeting all your requirements will give you confidence as you become accustomed to your new environment.

The length of your trip and your confidence level will determine how many nights you book in advance. You can always book a week or two in advance and cancel or change your reservations as needed. If you find a better place to stay from fellow travelers, you can always cancel. In those cases, you normally lose your 10% down payment unless you purchased cancellation insurance with your booking. Check booking agent conditions before booking. It is very easy to book hostels online while traveling. Be sure and ALWAYS ask to see the room and facilities before checking in and if not satisfied, ask for another room or seek other accommodations.

LOCAL TRANSPORTATION

In certain situations, it may be advisable to buy any internal airfare tickets and train tickets needed before traveling depending on demand and accessibility. You should also research all transportation options from the airport to your sleeping accommodations.

Internal airfare may be needed to connect to an ongoing destination upon arrival or soon thereafter. In this case, you do not want to rely on availability. In addition, if you are flying open-jaw, you may need a flight to get to your departure destination. You want to purchase that ticket as soon as possible to make sure you do not miss the connecting flight back home.

Train tickets such as Eurail, Orient-Express, Trans-Siberian Railway and others that are in great demand should be purchased in advance as soon as your travel dates are scheduled. Eurail passes can be purchased for specific travel periods and specific countries in Europe and are cheaper when purchased in the United States.

Most booking websites include directions from the airport to your sleeping destination on their confirmation and explain the transportation options available. Usually there are public buses, shuttles or trains from the airport to the town centre. Taxis are the most expensive mode of transportation from the airport. If it is necessary to take a taxi from the airport, make sure that the price has been negotiated in advance. Share a taxi with other travelers, if possible. In many cases, the hostel, guesthouse or budget hotel will pick you up at the airport. If not, they may be able to arrange a taxi to pick you up at a reduced rate and without the confusion of trying to explain directions to a cab driver in a foreign country. Always keep the name of your accommodation written on a piece of paper to give to the taxi driver.

BUDGETING AND MONEY

Travel guides provide budget travel estimates for each particular country. They give approximate costs in dollars for accommodations, food and transportation. These are based on the date of publication. These estimates do not include fees associated with tourist sights or activities. The budget cost provided will give you an idea of the minimum amount of money necessary for this trip when added to your airfare expense.

One of your first expenses when planning a trip should be to purchase a money belt. These can be worn under your clothes around the waist or neck. I prefer the ones worn around the waist and after wearing it for a while, you will no longer realize that you have it on. Money belts should be used to carry your passport, important documents, credit or debit cards and emergency cash. You should always take a few hundred dollars for emergencies in case you are unable to get funds from the ATM. It is easy to cash U.S. currency when traveling and is the currency of preference in many countries. You should go to the bank before traveling and get new bills that have no marking or writing on them. U.S. currency that is marked, old or written on is usually not accepted in foreign countries.

The easiest and safest way to travel with your money is by using credit and/or debit cards and ATMs. Find out what fees are associated with using them while traveling abroad. To reduce ATM fees you should withdraw larger amounts of cash each time rather than making numerous withdrawals of smaller amounts. Traveler's checks are almost obsolete because they are time consuming, expensive to cash and must be cashed during bank hours. ATMs are available 24 hours a day and available in almost every location that you visit. It is important to take

at least two debit and/or credit cards preferably one Visa and one Mastercard. Some
small towns or villages may only accept Visa
or MasterCard, not both. Keep them separate in case you lose one or one is stolen. It
is IMPORTANT that you notify your bank
and/or credit card company of the dates and
countries involved in your trip. If not, you
may find that your cards are not valid. You
should keep a list of phone numbers for your
bank or credit card company to call in case
your cards are lost or stolen. These numbers
are normally on the back of the card. Also,
keep a list of your debit and credit card numbers and expiration dates to provide if re-
quested by the bank or credit card company.
Be careful when using ATMs and make sure
that no one sees you using your pin number.
Do not use ATMs that are not well lit and
in a public area. I do not like to use ATMs
without watching someone successfully use it
first. Western Union has offices everywhere
and is an alternative to debit and credit cards
in an emergency.

Being able to manage your bank and
credit accounts online is very important.
Make sure that you have online accessibility
and are able to make payments and transfers

to all of your accounts. That way, if your debit card does not work for some reason, you can make payments to your credit card from your bank account and use it instead. Do not use your credit card for cash advances unless it is an emergency. Credit card companies charge excessive fees for cash advances. However, if you have to use your credit card for a cash advance, pay if off immediately via your bank account to keep them from charging the high interest charge for more than a day or so. If you have a savings account or money market account, it may be advisable to be able to transfer funds to your bank checking account. In addition, online access allows you to monitor both your checking and credit card accounts to make sure there are no false charges or that you were overcharged. If there was a false charge or you were overcharged, contact the bank immediately and dispute the charges. I check my accounts online at least every other day.

If you must use a currency exchange, look around for the best exchange rate available. Try to avoid currency exchanges at the airport. While they state they do not charge a fee to change currency, the exchange rate is so bad that you end up losing about 20%

on the exchange. I prefer to use all of my foreign currency remaining for the departure tax and buying gifts at the airport rather than paying the high commission. Use ATMs at the airport upon arrival for obtaining local currency instead of using the currency exchange.

Finally, it is very important to get used to the exchange rate for the foreign currency in comparison to the dollar. We think of things in dollars and for proper evaluation whether the price is reasonable, we must equate it in dollars. For instance, if traveling in Guatemala and they tell you the room is 80 quetzals, you should know that the current exchange rate is eight quetzals to a dollar and therefore the room is $10. Learning to do a quick currency conversion will be helpful while shopping, eating in a restaurant and almost every aspect of traveling. Some travelers like to make a small "cheat sheet" listing U.S. dollar amounts and their corresponding amounts in the local currency.

"WHEN PREPARING TO TRAVEL, LAY OUT ALL YOUR CLOTHES AND ALL YOUR MONEY. THEN TAKE HALF THE CLOTHES AND TWICE THE MONEY."
Susan Heller

Lake Atitlan, Guatemala

Tikal, Guatemala

TRAVEL INSURANCE

There are several types of travel insurance to be considered. There is supplemental medical insurance, flight cancellation insurance and insurance for personal property in case of loss or theft. The first thing you should do is see if your current medical insurance will cover you while traveling abroad. If not, you may want to consider supplemental medical coverage. Before buying any travel insurance, you should check with several companies for their types of coverage, the cost, and the requirements that must be met to collect. Many companies have very strict policies on what must occur in order to collect. After acquiring all the information, you must determine if the risk is worth the cost. The cost of your vacation, valuables that you will be traveling with and whether you are covered by your medical insurance will be among factors to consider before purchasing travel insurance.

BEFORE YOU LEAVE

Many things should be taken care of before you leave to ensure a worry free travel experience. Make sure all banks and credit card companies have been notified of your travel plans, all appliances have been turned off, mail and newspapers have been stopped, all pets have been taken care of and precautions taken to prevent your house from being burglarized. You may consider having a friend or relative housesit for you. Renting out your residence may be an option if you are going on an extended trip. Some travelers cut off the water to their home to keep from returning to a flooded home. Disconnect or suspend any services that you do not need and make sure you can pay those online that you would like to continue. If not, have a friend or relative pay any bills that must be paid. Finally, print out your boarding pass on your home computer before going to the airport. This is usually available 24 hours before departure. If you are traveling with only a carry-on, and you should be, you do not want to wait in line for 2 hours waiting to get your boarding pass if it is not necessary. While most airlines have kiosks at the airport to get your boarding passes; better safe than sorry. Try considering all possible situations that may occur while you are gone and have a plan in place to take care of these.

PACKING

Packing light is what all backpackers hope to achieve and that very few actually achieve. Ideally, you just need a good backpack, a few outfits of clothes, a good pair of hiking shoes, a camera, personal items, passport and money. You should always pack the same whether you are traveling for a week or six months. There is just more laundry involved when traveling for six months. It is very easy and inexpensive to do laundry in most countries. Unfortunately, the majority of us will pack too much and realize after the trip that we did not use everything in our backpack. Deciding what to take and what not to take is always a difficult decision. Decide whether you truly need an item before packing it. Most travel guides will tell you to place all the necessary items that you want to take on your trip on your bed and then cut that in half. Less is always better. You can easily buy clothes and toiletries while traveling. Packing light gives you mobility and eliminates those expensive airline baggage fees. Be sure and do several dry runs by packing what you intend to take in your backpack and walking around the neighborhood to see how it feels. There is no requirement that you fill up every square inch of your backpack. Remember that all liquids, gels and aerosols must be 3.4 ounces or less and fit within a single, clear quart-size Ziploc bag. The following are things I consider necessities which should be included in your backpack. I have also listed a few optional things to consider for your trip. Remember, no one later says I packed too little.

BACKPACK

Selecting the right backpack for you is the most important packing decision you will make. The backpack you have chosen and what you put into it will determine how comfortable you will be traveling. A sturdy and light backpack is always the best combination. It should be made of durable fabric and have several compartments for easy storage. Better quality backpacks usually translate to backpacks that are more comfortable. It should be approximately 9" X 14"X 22" or 45 linear inches (length + width + height) to qualify as carry-on luggage. Be sure to check weight allowances for your carry-on with your specific airline before flying. Do not forget, less is better. You are allowed one personal piece of luggage such as a purse, laptop, small backpack or camera in addition to your carry-on luggage. Your personal item must be 40-42 linear inches or less depending on the airline. You may opt for a traditional backpack or one that is a backpack with rollers, which allows you to pull it behind you. You should try on your backpack and adjust all the straps before your trip. It is also important to buy a rain cover for your backpack if one is not included. The last thing you want is to get all your possessions wet. Some backpacks may even include a waterproof interior liner as an extra precaution.

CLOTHING

When traveling to a warm or tropical region it is important to take lightweight clothes that dry easily especially since rain seems to appear from nowhere. When traveling to cooler or colder regions it is important to layer your clothes rather than take big, bulky coats. The following are what I consider essential clothing to include in your backpack. An important tip is to bring less and wash more often. This theme can't be repeated too often.

(a) GORE-TEX PARKA OR SIMILAR WATERPROOF SHELL - This outer shell can be used as a rain jacket in warm tropical weather and a windbreaker in colder weather. This has always been the most used piece of clothing in my backpack. My Gore-Tex has been to the summit of Kilimanjaro and deep in the Amazon jungle. This is also especially helpful on cold planes and colder buses in South America.

(b) SHORTS, SHIRTS, SKIRTS and PANTS- These should be color coordinated as much as possible to make as many possible matching combinations. Cotton clothing should not be taken to cooler or colder regions. T-shirts are great in tropical regions.

Several companies make lightweight pants that have zip off legs that can double as shorts. I always take old clothes in my backpack, which allows me to throw away clothes as needed and buy new inexpensive clothing. On the last day of my trip, I dispose of most of my old clothes and use the added space for souvenirs for family and friends. I do carry one nice pair of pants and one nice shirt for going out with my new backpacker friends. I always carry an empty 3-ounce spray mister, which can be found at Wal-Mart to remove wrinkles from my clothes. Simply fill the spray mister with water, hang up your clothes and spray a light mist of water over them. Within minutes, the weight of the water will remove the wrinkles and your clothes will be dry. Rolling your clothes before placing them in your backpack will take up less room than folding them. Rolling several pairs of pants and shirts together works the best. Placing plastic from the dry cleaner over your clothes before rolling them will help reduce wrinkling.

(c) SHOES, SOCKS and UNDERWEAR- 1 pair of shoes may be all you need for your trip. A good pair of waterproof cross-trainers can be used in warm, cool and cold regions.

If traveling in a warm climate, a good pair of sandals or flip-flops makes a great second pair of shoes. Flip flops are great shoes for the shower. Make sure that your shoes are broken in to prevent blisters. It is also advisable to carry extra shoelaces in case one of them breaks. Always wear your bulkiest shoes on the plane so you have more space in your backpack. Do not forget that the space inside your shoes is valuable packing space. Any socks that you take should be of good quality and provide wicking (removes moisture away from the skin). There is no need to take five pair of underwear on your trip. It is very easy to wash these in your sink along with anything else that dries easily.

(d) SWIMSUIT- If traveling in a warm region, include a swimsuit. My swimsuit doubles as an extra pair of shorts.

(e) GLOVES and WOOL CAP- Necessities if traveling in areas that are cold. I use a good pair of glove liners instead of bulky gloves.

ELECTRONICS

(a) DIGITAL CAMERA- A good digital camera with a zoom lens is a necessity for capturing those "once in a lifetime" moments.

One or two high capacity memory cards (4-gigabytes or larger) will keep you from having to download or get your pictures burned to a CD as often. Be sure to carry your battery charger and USB connector for uploading pictures to a computer if needed. You should also carry an extra set of batteries for your camera. Many cell phones now have great cameras that can be substituted instead of a traditional camera if you prefer.

(b) NETBOOK COMPUTER/TABLETS - (optional) The size, power and cost of the new netbook computers and tablets, such as i-Pad 2, make them a backpacker's friend. Most hostels have free internet and computers you may use but these are always busy. Internet cafes are inexpensive in most countries and easy to find but still there is a fee to get online. Netbook computers and tablets fit easily in your backpack and take advantage of the free Wi-Fi, which is accessible at every hostel and many restaurants and bars where backpackers congregate. It is so nice to have your own computer to use without waiting for someone else. I also use the netbook to download my pictures periodically as a backup. I strongly suggest that you take a netbook or tablet if you are traveling for an extended period.

(c) CELL PHONE/SMARTPHONE- (optional) With most young backpackers this is not an option but a necessity. Today's Smartphones give the backpacker internet access via Wi-Fi. While most international calling plans are too expensive to use while traveling, Skype allows those with Wi-Fi access to make free or inexpensive calls to friends and loved ones. Cell phones can come in very handy when you need to change or make travel reservations. An option is purchasing a sim card for the country you are visiting or buying a phone when arriving at your destination. You simply have to purchase usage as needed. The cost for this is very inexpensive. The Apps available for Smartphones such as foreign phrase translators or GPS can make traveling much easier. If you own a Smartphone or plan on buying one, make sure to find out the costs associated with using these Apps.

(d) BATTERY CHARGER and INTERNATIONAL VOLTAGE CONVERTER- I have rechargeable batteries for my camera, electric razor and flashlight. I would spend a fortune on batteries if I did not use rechargeable batteries. The international voltage converter allows those from the U.S. to plug in our electrical items into the electrical sockets of other countries through various adapters. A voltage kit will have adapter plugs that will fit all countries around the world.

(e) TRAVEL ALARM - A small travel alarm is essential for making early morning flights, trains or buses. A cell phone with an alarm feature can be substituted if you are carrying one with you.

Personal Items And Hygiene

- -

All liquid toiletries are limited to 3.4 ounces or less in carry-on luggage. They must fit within a single, clear quart-size sealable bag such as a Ziploc bag. Purchasing empty 3.4 ounce bottles and filling them with your own products is a cheaper option than purchasing travel size toiletries.

(a) TOILET PAPER- Other than money and my passport, I consider this the most essential thing to pack. I keep toilet paper in a Ziploc bag to keep it from getting wet and to make it easy to find. There will be a situation on almost every trip where you have to rely on your own supply. Tissue packets are easy to find and handy to keep in your backpack.

(b) SHAMPOO and CONDITIONER- Take a combination 3.4 ounce or less travel size shampoo/conditioner to use upon your arrival and then buy a larger size when no longer flying. A cheaper option is to fill an empty 3 ounce bottle with your own shampoo. Empty travel bottles can be found at Wal-Mart.

(c) TOOTHBRUSH and TOOTHPASTE- 3.4 ounces or less. Buy larger size after arriving at your destination, when needed. The same brands are available in almost every country.

(d) BRUSH and/or COMB- A small folding travel brush and/or comb.

(e) FEMININE HYGIENE PRODUCTS- Most feminine hygiene products can be purchased everywhere in the world but do your research to make sure.

(f) DEODORANT- Liquid or gel deodorant must be 3.4 ounces or less but solid deodorant can be any size in your carry-on. Only take what you need.

(g) HAIR DRYER - This may be optional for some and a necessity for others. If a necessity, take a small travel hair dryer or rent one at the hostel.

(h) SOAP- A small 3.4 ounce or less bottle of concentrated soap is good for bathing and laundry done in the sink.

(i) CONTACT LENSES, READING or PRESCRIPTION GLASSES- It is always best to take an extra pair. Contact solution must be in bottles 3.4 ounces or less.

(j) SUNGLASSES- Preferably an inexpensive pair with UV protection that you will not worry about losing.

(k) RAZOR- I like the electric travel razor but any kind will do. Disposable razors and razor blades can be purchased everywhere.

(l) MANICURE SET- Nail clippers and tweezers always come in handy but remember no scissors with a blade 4 inches or longer allowed in carry-on luggage.

MEDICINE

You will be able to locate a pharmacy wherever you are traveling but I always keep a few things in my bag for convenience.

(a) FIRST-AID KIT- Just take the basics, anything else can be purchased at the local pharmacy.

(b) ANTIBIOTICS- You never need them until you need them.

(c) PRESCRIPTIONS- Make sure the medicine is in its original bottle and the labels are legible.

(d) PAIN RELIEVER- Ibuprofen

(e) ALLERGY MEDICINE- It never fails, when I don't have it, I need it.

(f) MALARIA TABLETS- Depending on your destination.

(g) SLEEP MEDICATION- For those long plane rides.

(h) DIARRHEA MEDICATION- Better safe than sorry.

MISCELLANEOUS

- -

(a) PAPERBACK NOVEL and PLAYING CARDS- For the long wait at airline terminal, train or bus stations or for the hostel lounge area.

(b) JOURNAL and INK PENS- Keeping a journal to recount my trip is something I believe everyone should do. Just a few lines each night about the day's activities will lead to many fond memories years later. I use my journal as a reference when I update my blog. Be sure to keep a pen handy on the plane for filling out immigration and custom forms.

(c) PICTURES of FAMILY- I always keep family pictures in my journal so I can look at them while jotting down the days activities.

(d) SNACKS in BACKPACK- These will come in handy while at the airport (astronomical food prices at the airport), while hiking or late night at the hostel.

(e) EMPTY WATER BOTTLE- Once again, this comes in handy at the airport terminal. You cannot bring drinks through the security checkpoints. Instead, bring an empty water bottle through security and fill it up at one of the many water fountains inside. This is a much better option than paying $3.00 for a 12 ounce bottled water or soda.

(f) INSECT REPELLENT- Make sure it is 3.4 ounces or less. Insect repellent is available abroad but the quality is usually less and it may be more expensive.

(g) MONEY BELT- I prefer the ones that you wear around your waist and under your clothes but those that hang around your neck are available. They take a little getting used to but the inconvenience is better than having your passport and money stolen.

(h) FLASHLIGHT or TORCH- A small flashlight comes in handy at times. Do not forget extra batteries.

(i) ZIPLOC BAGS - Take several. They can be used for lot of things.

(j) PADLOCK- A small padlock will help keep your stuff safe in your dorm locker. I prefer a combination lock so I do not have to worry about keeping up with a key.

(k) EARPLUGS- This can be helpful on the plane or for any late night noise in the hostel.

(l) DUCT TAPE- Wrap a few feet around an ink pen. You will be surprised how often it comes in handy.

(m) SHEET OF FABRIC SOFTENER- Place a sheet of fabric softener in your backpack when packing. It absorbs odors and dampness and keeps clothing smelling fresh.

(n) TWIST TIE- Keep a twist tie in your wallet or backpack. It can be used to temporarily repair glasses if the screw falls out. Just peel off the paper or plastic so you have bare wire and insert it where the screw was and twist to tighten.

(o) KEY CHAIN OR BINER- A key chain or biner can be used to latch the zippers together on a backpack. This will make it difficult for a thief to remove things from your backpack while at a busy train or bus station.

DOCUMENTS

It is important to make copies of your passport and important documents. Keep them separate from the originals. You should also leave a copy of these documents with family or friends.

(a) PASSPORT- Make sure it is valid, will not expire while you are traveling and has enough blank pages for visas.

(b) PASSPORT PHOTOS FOR VISAS- Some countries require that you have an extra passport photo to obtain a visa.

(c) VACCINATION CERTIFICATE- If required at your travel destination.

(d) CREDIT/DEBIT CARD INFO- Keep a list of your card numbers and their expiration dates along with contact numbers. I keep this info in an email sent to myself.

(e) LIST of IMPORTANT ADDRESSES and PHONE NUMBERS- Your journal is a good place to keep them or in an email file.

(f) HEALTH and TRAVEL INSURANCE INFORMATION- Keep a list of all policy numbers and contact information.

WHAT NOT TO PACK

- -

(a) Expensive jewelry
(b) Your entire beauty routine
(c) More than one Guidebook
(d) Travel iron (use spray mister)
(e) Anything you can buy at your destination

FINAL REVIEW

- -

Look back through your backpack and determine if each item is necessary. If you are not sure, leave it home. If it can be purchased at your destination, it is not necessary. PACK LESS, WASH MORE.

CHAPTER 10

TRAVELING

> "AS YOU WALK AND EAT AND TRAVEL, BE
> WHERE YOU ARE, OTHERWISE YOU WILL MISS MOST
> OF YOUR LIFE."
>
> *Buddha*

When traveling to a foreign country, it is very important to know how the country's language will affect you. Is English widely spoken? It is also important to know the types of local transportation offered, sleeping accommodations available and where to eat to stay on budget. Travel guides are an excellent source for this information.

109

Hostelworld.com and hostels.com also provide selected city guides on their websites. Information available on these selected cities includes things to see, entertainment, where to eat and transport. There is also some general information on the destination.

LANGUAGE DIFFICULTIES???

Usually the first question that I am asked by those who have not traveled abroad is, "How can you travel to a country that speaks a foreign language?" Most of them surmise that I, like a majority of Americans, only speak English. Luckily, the rest of the world has realized the importance of learning English when business and tourist dollars are at risk. From cab drivers to shop merchants, almost everyone associated with tourism can speak some English in almost every country. Only while traveling in China after the 2008 Olympics did I truly have language difficulty. There was a huge effort before the Olympics to learn English but it was still in the beginning stages. The majority still did not speak English but they were quickly learning. Those in China who did speak some English would seek me out to practice. It is very helpful to have your hostel write down your intended destination for cab drivers or to help in purchasing train or bus tickets. Many signs are in both English and the country's language in most countries. It is always best to learn a few important foreign phrases or words while traveling, though not necessary. Most guidebooks have important travel phrases and words in a language section in the back of the book. I always use flashcards before my trip to learn words that I believe will be useful. Many restaurants will have menus in English but usually these are "tourist' restaurants and more expensive. Some of my funniest moments traveling have come while trying to order food in foreign countries. This includes clucking and flapping my arms like a chicken, much to the amusement of my waitress in Peru.

Floating Islands of Lake Titicaca in Peru

Proficiency in charades is helpful when there is a communication problem. When all else fails, I have found that smiling and pointing are universal and understood by all. Traveling in a foreign country is also a great opportunity to learn a new language or improve your current language skills. There are many courses that are geared especially for backpackers and which are inexpensive. Some of these include homestays in which there is no English spoken (Immersion). This includes not only language lessons but also room and board.

LOCAL TRANSPORTATION

Local transportation includes regional airlines, trains, buses and minibuses, boats and ferries, metro or subway, taxis, rental cars, camper vans, tour buses, bikes and walking.

(a) REGIONAL AIRLINES- Regional airlines sometimes offer a viable alternative to buses and trains when traveling depending on the country or region you are visiting. Sometimes a flight that saves you a lot of travel time is worth the additional cost. There are even certain times that a flight is cheaper than bus or train travel. A bus from

Ushuaia, Argentina to Buenos Aires took 50 hours and cost $300. A flight from Ushuaia to Buenos Aires was only $250. It did not take me long to decide which mode of travel to use. Be sure to check your Travel Guides to see which regional airlines fly to your destination.

(b) TRAINS- Depending on the countries you are visiting and the distance you will be traveling, trains can be a fun and economic alternative. Traveling through Europe on a Eurail Pass is a great way to visit many countries and train travel in China is one of the least expensive ways to travel. Another advantage of train travel is that you arrive in the town centre. This eliminates the expense of getting into the city from the airport, which can be substantial. Most travelers stay near the town centre, which is the hub of tourist activity.

Sleeper trains allow you to travel great distances while saving a night's accommodation. While traveling through Europe, I would always try to take the overnight sleeper train when possible. There is nothing better than spending the day and evening in Paris, boarding the train and waking up bright and early in Madrid.

Paris from Notre Dame Cathedral

Trains, like buses, offer many departure and arrival times, which allows more latitude in planning your trip. It is always better to arrive at your next destination at a reasonable and safe hour.

Train tickets come in different classes with different prices. You should check the train's website to find out the differences and prices of these classes. Sleeper cars also come in different prices depending on the class and number of bunks in your room. I traveled in a 2nd class sleeper while traveling through China. It was much cheaper than 1st class and the major differences were two extra bunks in the room and no door to the hallway. At first, I was concerned by the lack of privacy by not having a door, but once the lights went out there was no problem.

It was a great experience and even though few Chinese spoke English, there was a lot of smiling and sharing of food. I suggest that you do not pick the bottom bunk when traveling by sleeper car. The bottom bunk always seems to be where all the passengers congregate to talk and eat, even on your bunk. The top bunk can be very difficult to climb into and may only have a minimum of space above you. This leaves the 2nd level bunk as usually the best option.

If you are planning to do a lot of traveling by train, you should get a map and train schedule to help in your planning. Be aware that even if you have a Eurail Pass, some tickets have to be reserved and involve an extra fee. In many cases, your hostel, guesthouse or budget hotel can assist in getting your train tickets for the next destination. If I am purchasing the tickets myself, I always ask the hostel to write down the destination and departure time in the foreign language in case they do not speak English.

(c) BUSES- Bus travel is usually the least expensive way to travel while backpacking. Buses also allow accessibility to regions that are not available by other means. There are many types of buses such as international buses, sleeper buses, intercity buses, mini-buses and shuttles, the infamous "chicken" buses, and city buses.

International buses travel from country to country and come in different classes (1st or 2nd) and prices. They may include many differing levels of comfort such as air conditioning, sleeper seats, reclining seats, food, toilets and movies. Most international buses, especially those in South America, are cold. (Really cold) Be prepared with jackets and/ or blankets. All locals come prepared with blankets on these buses. Not all of these comforts may be included on all international buses. You should check with your hostel, local travel company, bus station or the buses website before purchasing your ticket to know what is included. Most cities and towns have several bus stations. Usually, international buses have their own station, so make sure you go to the right station to catch your bus.

Sleeper buses may be international or national depending on the size of the country. My first sleeper bus was within China and my second experience was a 28 hour ride from China to Laos. Sleeper buses are easily to distinguish because they have either single or double beds instead of seats. Your bed is your seat for the duration of the trip. They normally have air conditioning and movies, though in my experience there was no toilet. Be sure to check and see what amenities are offered before purchasing your ticket.

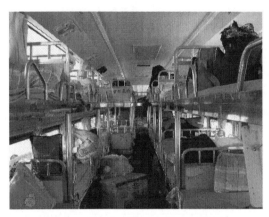

Sleeper bus in Kunming, China

Intercity buses travel to most areas within the country. In many cases, there are 1st or 2nd class options. These buses depart and connect the major cities and towns of a country. Once again, these buses can be very cold so be prepared. The http://thebusschedule. com provides an online bus schedule for those traveling in Mexico, Central and South America and the Caribbean.

Minibuses and shuttles offer an alternative to regular bus travel. They vary greatly from country to country. Some are very nice, expensive and must be reserved. Others, however, are unbelievably cheap. These are easy to spot due to someone hanging out the door of the van shouting their next destination. People are getting in and out of the van continuously as the "hawkers" try to keep the van full. It is quite the experience and very commonplace in Central and South America.

Without a doubt, my favorite traveling experience is riding the "chicken bus". These are retired, yellow American school buses that have been shipped to Central America to prolong their usefulness. The buses have normally been painted several vibrant colors and adorned with various decorations. They travel from short distances to several hours connecting remote towns and regions where more "conventional" buses do not travel. They are called "chicken buses" because it is not uncommon to see chickens or produce riding along with passengers on their way to market. There is nothing more exciting that riding the mountain roads in Guatemala in a bus deemed by the U.S. as too old to remain in service. It is an experience that every traveler must try, at least once.

"Chicken bus" in Antigua, Guatemala

Antigua, Guatemala

City buses are the cheapest way to get around cities and towns unless there is a subway or metro. Hostels usually provide bus routes, including bus numbers for all important tourist attractions. Watch your valuables.

Bus stations, like train stations, are usually located near the town centre. This is ideal for the backpacker since most hostels are located near the town centre. Cities and towns usually have several bus stations that are designated for certain routes and bus companies. If you are planning to travel by bus, make sure you know from which station you will depart. Your Travel Guide will most likely have a list of bus stations and towns they service. Your hostel is probably the best source of this information and the bus schedules. Bus stations are like mini-cities. There are food stalls and markets everywhere. Depending on the length of your bus trip, it is always a good idea to purchase some food and drink for the trip. At every stop, vendors will usually board the bus with food and drink for sale. There will be breaks to use the restroom and purchase food if the bus ride is very long.

I never store my baggage in the bus compartments or on top of the "chicken bus". One of the advantages of traveling with just a backpack is keeping it with you all the time. I ride with my bag in my lap. While this may be uncomfortable, it is much easier than watching the luggage compartment every time the bus stops to make sure no one takes your bag. I knew a backpacker in Ecuador who placed his bag in the overhead compartment above his seat only to find it was stolen by the first stop. Another couple were told not to hold their bag but to put it under their seat for safety by a local sitting behind them. When they got off the bus, they realized their bag had been cut and all the valuables were stolen. If you ride enough local or chicken buses, someone will try to steal your backpack or valuables. Be careful with your possession all the time.

(d) BOATS and FERRIES- Boats and ferries play an important role in local transportation. In many instances, they provide accessibility to an otherwise difficult destination. Boats provide backpackers access to trips up and down rivers such as the Amazon, Yangtze or Mekong. It would not be economically possible to travel around the Greek Isles without the use of ferries. Ferries are also an inexpensive way to see harbors, such as the ones in Sydney and Hong Kong without paying the price for an expensive tour. Anytime you are considering a boat tour, check to see if there is a ferry with a similar route.

(e) METRO or SUBWAY- If staying in a big city, the metro or subway is one of the most budget-friendly ways to travel. There are usually passes available to suit the number of days you will be visiting the city. Some city passes give discounts for buses, metro and museums. Be sure to stay aware of the closing hours of the metro and realize that you may have to pay for a taxi if staying out late.

(f) TAXIS- Taxis are my least favorite mode of transportation but sometimes a necessity. If there is no public transportation available or it is late at night, it may be necessary to take a taxi. If this is the case, try to find someone to share the cost. Taxis are also a good idea if you are planning a late night out due to its safety. Taking a bus or the metro late at night might be dangerous. If the taxi is not using a meter, be sure to set the price before getting in the taxi. Never put your backpack in the trunk. I have heard horror stories of the taxi driver trying to charge more than the agreed upon price and using the baggage in the trunk as a hostage. Be sure and keep the hostel's business card with you, in case there is a communication problem with the driver.

(g) CAR RENTAL- I am not a fan of car rental due to the expense of the rental, parking, gas and insurance. Be aware of additional fees and taxes, which sometimes can increase your base rate by 40%. Parking a rental car can sometimes be very difficult and expensive. Check the fine print closely before renting. I like to enjoy the scenery while traveling by bus or train without the worry of driving. However, you might want to consider the option of a car depending on the number of travelers in your group and your destination. In many cases, this may be a good option. On occasion, I have seen several backpackers put a group together at the hostel and rent a car for the day to see the sights.

(h) CAMPER VANS- Camper vans are big in New Zealand and Australia and provide both transportation and sleeping accommodations. These are a great alternative for those who enjoy camping.

(i) TOUR BUSES- City tour buses that allow get on, get off access throughout the day can be great for the budget. It is similar to a guided tour but without the restrictions. I like the fact that you can get off at the attractions that you are interested in seeing and then catch the next tour bus that comes by. It does not force you to spend time seeing those sights that do not interest you.

(j) BIKES- European cities such as Copenhagen, Amsterdam, Munich and Paris have hundreds of miles of bike paths and numerous bike rental stations. For instance, Velib' in Paris has 750 rental locations with over 20,000 bicycles at a price of less than $1.50 per hour. In smaller towns, bikes are a great way to tour the countryside. There are also many tours exclusively for biking. One of my most exciting adventures was riding a mountain bike down the "Death Road" in Bolivia. The guided bike trip descended over 12,000 feet along 40 miles of dirt road. There were no guardrails and it was a 2000-foot drop at most points. I also participated in a bike tour through the vineyards of Mendoza, Argentina combined with a wine tasting tour. The bikes were placed on a trailer for the return trip back to Mendoza, as a safety precaution.

Bill Passman

Biking the "Death Road" in Bolivia

"Death Road" in Bolivia

(k) WALKING- This is my favorite form of local transportation and should be used whenever possible. Instead of taking one of the many buses along the traffic infested Ring of Kerry in Ireland, I chose to hike the Kerry Way instead. The trip was hostel to hostel and took 7 days but involved seeing sights and experiencing the culture that one does not get from a bus tour.

Walking instead of taking the bus or a taxi can also help keep you on budget. There are many instances where you can walk to the hostel from the bus or train station rather than take a taxi. These savings quickly add up over a long trip. If it is late at night or you have not packed light, then maybe a taxi is your only option. Before taking any other local transportation, ask yourself if it is close enough to walk.

Hiking the Ring of Kerry in Ireland

SLEEPING

If traveling on a budget, you are most likely to stay at a hostel (dorm or private room), family guesthouse, or budget hotel. If traveling by yourself, dorms are the most economical. However, a family guesthouse in Southeast Asia, Central or South America can also be incredibly inexpensive. On recent trip to the island of Koh Lanta in Thailand, I was able to get a private room with air conditioning, queen size bed, cable television, private bath with hot water and refrigerator for only $7.00 a night. The room was only a two-minute walk to the beach. If traveling with one or more people private rooms can be almost as inexpensive per person as a dorm bed.

Another option, many hostels are always looking for travelers willing to work a few hours a day in exchange for accommodations and food. Also, many PADI dive shops are an excellent place to inquire about inexpensive accommodations.

The most inexpensive accommodations are camping and couch surfing. Camping requires carrying all the gear needed for sleeping including a tent and sleeping bag along with cooking utensils and food. Many hostels allow campers to camp on their property for a reduced fee and still allow them use of the hostel's amenities. CouchSurfing is fairly new. CouchSurfing is a worldwide network for making connections between travelers and the local communities they visit. Additional information regarding CouchSurfing can be found at couchsurfing.org.

Internet sites such as hostelworld.com, hostels.com, hihostel.com and hostelbookers.com provide information to find not only hostels but also family guesthouses and budget hotels.

The information provided by these sites includes prices, availability, facilities, photos, reviews, ratings, maps & directions for hostels, guesthouses and budget hotels. The ratings include character, security, location, staff, fun and cleanliness. Reviews are important because it gives you a firsthand perspective from someone who has recently stayed at that particular accommodation. I usually pick hostels with the highest security and location ratings when compared to other hostels with similar ratings. The photos give you an opportunity to look at the hostel including the room accommodations and bathroom facilities. These websites will automatically check availability once you enter the dates that you need the room. Prices depend on the quality of the accommodation and whether a dorm or private room is selected.

These sites also provide booking and confirmation after you have selected where and when you plan to stay. Be sure to print out your confirmation and keep a copy in your email folder. The confirmation will provide directions from the airport, train or bus station to the hostel, family guesthouse or budget hotel. It also includes the address and phone number which are very helpful, especially if you need to take a taxi.

Guidebooks also provide a list of accommodations but their information is only accurate as of the guide's publication date.

It is also a good idea to do an internet search for hostels at your destination. Many hostels are not listed on hostelworld.com, hostels.com or the other popular websites. In addition, combine an online search with a phone call or email asking if there is a possibility of a reduced rate.

How far in advance to book your reservation depends on whether you are traveling in the peak season and the popularity of the accommodation. If traveling in the peak season book all accommodations as far in advance as possible. At other times, you need only book a few days in advance. Check the availability at the hostel websites frequently to monitor how quickly the hostels are filling up.

There is always a sense of adventure when one does not make a reservation in advance. Many wonderful hostels, family guesthouses and budget hotels are not listed in guidebooks or websites. You will learn of many of these from other backpackers and some you will find by accident. Sometimes when arriving in a new town early in the day I will walk around looking at different hostels. This gives me an opportunity to see them firsthand and negotiate the price. Whether arriving by train, bus or boat, there is always someone with brochures touting their accommodations. They are paid a commission to bring travelers to their hostel or guesthouse. Some of my favorite hostels were found this way. Be careful, many taxi drivers will tell you that the hostel you are looking for is no longer in business. Then they can take you to a hostel that pays them a commission in addition to the cab fare. Looking through a guidebook while in a taxi is a sure-fire way to let the cabdriver know that you have no reservation.

After arriving at your accommodation, ask to see the room and other facilities before paying. If you are not satisfied, ask for another room or find another place. Many hostels will overbook and try to accommodate travelers with inferior rooms close by. Before arriving, it is always helpful to reconfirm your reservation and make sure to bring a copy of your confirmation.

> "TO AWAKEN IN A STRANGE TOWN IS ONE OF THE MOST PLEASANT SENSATIONS IN THE WORLD."
>
> *Freya Stark*

EATING

One must eat inexpensively if they plan to stay on budget. This can be done by eating at the hostel, local restaurants, and day or night markets.

The best way to save money while traveling is taking advantage of the community kitchens in most hostels. They provide stoves, refrigerators, cooking utensils, plates, cups and silverware. Your responsibility is to clean up your mess, throw away all trash and wash your dishes. It is much cheaper to buy food at the market than to eat out every night. Everyone labels their food and drinks and places them in the pantry or refrigerator. It can be a little crazy in the kitchen sometimes with several people cooking at once but it is just another one of those backpacking experiences. Sandwiches, cereal and spaghetti seem to be backpacker favorites no matter where you are in the world. In addition, many hostels provide a free breakfast. This normally consists of toast, jam, cereal, fruit, juice and coffee. The majority of hostels in Southeast Asia do not have community kitchens due to the low cost of food in day and night markets and local restaurants. It would be more expensive to cook a meal than eat at one of those.

Local restaurants are the restaurants where the locals eat, not the tourist restaurants. You can tell a tourist restaurant by the sign that says, "We speak English". They also will have an English menu and very few locals eating there. In Central and South America, you should ask for the "set" lunches at the local restaurants. These usually include your choice of meat, vegetables, soup, bread and drink for a very small price. Any restaurants close to the town centre will be tourist oriented and very expensive. Try a few blocks away from the town centre and look for a restaurant crowded with locals and few tourists. This will be where the best and least expensive food is located.

Day and night markets are my favorite places to eat. There are stalls of vendors as far as the eye can see cooking almost everything imaginable. Grilled meat, especially chicken, seems to be a favorite all over the world. While many may have a concern for safety, seeing your food being cooked over an open flame is probably as safe as one can expect. The food in day and night markets is unbelievably cheap. In Southeast Asia, these markets are continuously busy and crowded. People seem to be eating from morning to night.

Day market in Laos

KEEPING IN TOUCH

The easiest ways to keep in touch with family and friends while traveling are the internet and cell phones. Pay phones are also readily available in many countries outside the United States.

(a) INTERNET- The internet is the most common and inexpensive way to keep in touch. This is done through Facebook, Skype, blogging, and email. Many backpackers carry their own netbook, tablet or Smartphone to take advantage of the numerous Wi-Fi outlets including hostels, airports, cafes and various municipal locations. Those without a computer can use the hostel's computer or one of the many Internet Cafes around the world.

Facebook has changed the way we keep in touch with everyone. Almost everyone has a Facebook account and checks it several times a day. It is so easy to quickly post how you are doing and at the same time see how everyone else is doing. It is also easy to post pictures of your travels. This is by far the most used way to keep in touch. WARNING: Do not spend all day in the hostel on Facebook telling your family and friends what a great time you are having.

Get out, see the sights and enjoy the culture. Too often, I see travelers on Facebook for hours each day instead of taking advantage of their travel opportunity.

Skype is quickly becoming a favorite of backpackers. Skype is software that enables individuals to make free video and voice calls to other Skype users from computer/Smartphone to computer/Smartphone. It is great to be able to see and hear loved ones and friends after traveling for an extended period. Skype can also be used to make low-cost calls from your computer to landlines and cell phones. More information can be found at skype.com.

Blogging is another easy way to keep in touch while traveling. A blog is a personal website, which can be dedicated to your trip if you like. You must first set up an account with someone like blogger.com. Blogging allows you to document and update your travels on a blog journal and post pictures for your family and friends. It involves much more depth and allows for more detail than a Facebook message or email would allow. In essence, it becomes a permanent record of your trip with narration and photos documenting every aspect of your trip. After setting up your blog, you give your blog site to family and friends. Then they can follow your travels whenever they wish. This keeps you from having to email everyone separately. It is also more private than Facebook. You should always set up a blog account and practice blogging and uploading pictures before your trip. This will give you an opportunity to iron out any problems that may occur.

Not long ago, email was the primary method of keeping in touch other than by phone. Facebook seems to have taken over most of our social connection. Email is still the most private way for us to send and receive messages. It is also sometimes necessary to use email when some of our friends and family, like my brother, do not have Facebook accounts.

(b) CELL PHONES/SMARTPHONES- Cell phones were once considered too expensive to use while traveling abroad. U.S. carriers have reduced their rates and now it is a viable alternative for limited use. Make sure to check with your carrier and find out the costs associated with cell phone use abroad. Many carriers may have texting plans that are available specifically for outside the United States. You may also bring your own unlocked international phone and purchase a sim card for that particular country. An alternative to bringing your own phone is purchasing one when you arrive at your destination. The prices are usually very reasonable and cell minutes can be purchased inexpensively almost everywhere. The decision on whether to buy one at your destination may also depend upon how long you will be in that country and if the phone works in other countries. Finally, if you have a Smartphone it can be used for internet access through the many Wi-Fi hotspots around the world. Doing your research regarding costs and ease of use is necessary in finding which option is best for you. Be sure to turn off data roaming on your Smartphone to block email, browsing, downloads and apps.

(c) PAY PHONES- While antiquated and seldom found in the U.S. anymore, many pay phones can be found while traveling abroad. Most usually require you to purchase a prepaid card before using. Some hostels still have pay phones that use credit cards or local currency. This comes in handy when there is no other option.

HEALTH

Making sure you have a healthy trip should be at the top of everyone's list. The following are steps that can be taken to keep you healthy and help in case you get ill.

(a) MEDICAL INSURANCE- Most U.S. plans do not provide coverage while traveling overseas. The ones that do provide coverage require you to pay the fees upfront and reimburse you later. You may want to check into the benefits of travel medical insurance before traveling abroad if your policy does not cover you.

(b) GET IN SHAPE- Make sure that you are physically in shape for your trip, especially if there is a lot of hiking or physical activity.

(c) SEE A DOCTOR- You may consider getting a physical or general checkup before leaving the country.

(d) VISIT YOUR DENTIST- If you need any dental work that needs to be performed, you may want to consider having it done before you leave.

(e) PRESCRIPTION MEDICINES- You should get any refills necessary and these should be in their original bottles with legible writing.

(f) VACCINATIONS- Be sure to research your destination for possible infectious diseases. Make sure that you have gotten all vaccinations required and that you have proper documentation to carry with you.

(g) PRE-EXISTING CONDITIONS- A traveler going abroad with a preexisting medical condition should carry a letter from the attending physician, describing the medical condition and any prescription medications, including the generic names of the prescribed drugs.

(h) WHILE ON A FLIGHT- The following will help keep you healthy on your flight.
- Don't touch eyes, nose or mouth.
- Bring travel-size bottle of hand sanitizer to use after washing hands in lavatory.
- Stay hydrated.
- Order drinks without ice.
- Get up and walk around every hour to stretch legs.

SAFETY

The U.S. Department of State has a very good website at www.travel.state.gov/ that provides important information regarding passports, visas, travel warnings and alerts and tips for traveling abroad safely.

The following is a partial list of safety tips found on their website. Go to the website for the complete list.

BEFORE YOU GO

(a) Safety begins when you pack. To help avoid becoming a target, do not dress as to mark yourself as an affluent tourist. (Usually not a problem for a backpacker) Expensive-looking jewelry, for instance, can draw the wrong attention.

(b) Always travel light. You can move more quickly and will be more likely to have a free hand.

(c) Don't bring anything you would hate to lose.

(d) Leave a copy of your itinerary with family and friends in case they need to contact you in case of emergency.

SAFETY ON THE STREETS

Use the same common sense traveling overseas that you would at home. Be especially cautious in (or avoid) areas where you may easily be victimized. These include crowded subways, train stations, elevators, tourist sites, market places and crime-ridden neighborhoods.

(a) Don't use shortcuts, narrow alleys or poorly lit streets.

(b) Do not travel alone at night.

(c) Avoid public demonstrations and other civil disturbances.

(d) Keep a low profile and avoid loud conversations or arguments.

(e) Do not discuss travel plans or other personal matters with strangers.

(f) Avoid scam artists by being wary of strangers who approach you and offer to be your guide or sell you something at a bargain price.

(g) Be aware of pickpockets, they often have an accomplice who will:
- Jostle you
- Ask for directions or the time
- Point to something spilled on your clothes
- Or distract you by creating a disturbance

(h) Try to seem purposeful when you move about. Even if you are lost, act as if you know where you are going. Try to ask for directions from individuals in authority.

(i) Do not accept food or drink from strangers.

(j) If you are confronted, don't fight back-give up your valuables.

MY SAFETY TIPS

(a) When taking a taxi make sure that the fare is completely understood before departing to your destination if a meter is not being used. Keep your backpack with you inside the taxi, if possible, even if they insist on placing it in the trunk. On occasion, taxi drivers have refused to return luggage without the passenger paying a greater fare than was agreed.

(b) While traveling on a local bus, it is always best to keep your backpack near you or in your lap. If you are unable, sit near a window near the luggage compartment and watch the luggage being unloaded to make sure no one steals your baggage. Thieves on buses have stolen luggage placed above the traveler and under their seats. When traveling on local transportation it is not if someone will try to steal your luggage, but when.

(c) Make sure to stay at hostels that have 24-hour security and are located in a safe neighborhood. If staying in a dorm make sure to lock your valuables in the locker provided. Be sure to bring your own padlock.

(d) Keep copies of credit/debit card information along with the banks telephone numbers in case your cards are stolen or lost. The information should include card numbers and expiration dates.

(e) Always use a money belt to keep valuable documents such as your passport and emergency U.S. dollars. Keep small amounts of currency in your pockets or a travel wallet so you do not have to show your money belt in public.

(f) If there are any problems contact the nearest U.S. Embassy. The address and phone number will be listed in your travel guide.

BEING A GOOD TRAVELER

Tourism is the world's fastest growing industry. With travel comes responsibility. We must ensure that our activities do not affect or destroy the very culture and environment of those countries we seek to visit. Travel to foreign countries is not a right but a privilege bestowed upon us by that country. It is our duty to respect that privilege by being a good traveler. A good traveler respects the country's culture, customs, environment and people.

You should research and learn as much as possible about the customs and culture of those countries that you plan to visit. This will help us understand the people and keep us from unintentionally disrespecting them.

For example, in Muslim countries, use only your right hand for eating and greeting, never your left. You should experience the culture by enjoying the food, shopping in the markets and attending local festivals.

Next, it is important as a good traveler to respect the environment. Do not litter and respect the country's flora and fauna. You would not want someone to put trash in your back yard and neither do they. You should remove any excessive packing material from recent purchases before you put them in your backpack. I will never forget a hiking trip to Everest Base Camp in 2007. The people were warm and friendly and the scenery was breathtaking. On the other hand, it was heartbreaking to witness the trash littered along the mountain trails by the hordes of tourist and tourist guides.

> "TAKE ONLY PICTURES. LEAVE ONLY FOOTPRINTS.
> KILL ONLY TIME."
> *Mark Vjuyen Jones*

New Zealand has a strict policy for hiking in the mountains. You pack it in; you pack it out. That includes not only trash but also any food you cooked and did not eat. Make sure we leave the environment as we found it or better so that our children and grandchildren may also appreciate it. Be careful when buying souvenirs. You do not want to buy anything made from flora, fauna or endangered wildlife.

The final step in being a good traveler is to respect the people of that country. Respect the differences and embrace the similarities in our cultures. Be courteous. Remember that, while traveling, you are a goodwill ambassador for your country and should act so. Learn a few words or phrases in the local language. Saying hello, please or thank you can go a long way to showing that you respect their culture. Refrain from aggressive bargaining. While bargaining is expected in most countries, remember they also have to make a living and support their families. Support locally owned businesses, community tour operators and artisans. This assures that your money will remain in the community. You should also be careful about giving things to children who are begging. While in Tanzania, I gave pens and pencils to the children outside our hotel. I later found out that the children would stay home from school to beg from the tourists. It would have been more productive for me to give supplies to the local school instead of the children. This would remove their incentive to miss school. It is also very important not to take pictures of locals without their permission, especially children. This is very disrespectful.

COMING BACK HOME

> "HE WHO RETURNS FROM A JOURNEY IS NOT
> THE SAME AS HE WHO LEFT."
>
> *Chinese Proverb*

This was a difficult chapter to write because the emotions evoked upon returning home will be different for everyone. However, I felt it was necessary to illustrate some of the contradictory feelings that may occur upon returning home, especially after a long trip.

Backpacking occurs at different stages in people's lives. Many backpack when they are young before it is necessary to make a living and raise a family. Others try to incorporate backpacking into their busy lives of family and work. Finally, many enjoy backpacking when they are older, have already raised their family and no longer have that responsibility. One thing is true in each situation, the more you travel, the more you want to travel. There are always mixed emotions upon returning from a trip. On one hand, there is the excitement of being home with family, friends and familiar surroundings. On the other hand, there is a feeling of boredom due to the lack of new and exciting people, places and things that you experience while traveling. Everyday on the road is a new adventure. A regular routine at home can quickly become a backpacker's worst nightmare.

> "I TRAVEL A LOT; I HATE HAVING MY LIFE DISRUPTED BY ROUTINE."
> *Caskie Stinnett*

I cannot think of anything more exciting and heartwarming than to have family and friends meet you at the airport after a long trip. Everyone is excited to see you and hear all the stories about your trip. The love and affection for family and friends seems to multiply tenfold while traveling and the anticipation of seeing them again is almost unbearable at times. It is true; absence makes the heart grow fonder. My grandchildren, Kade and Madison, are usually asking after a few weeks when I will be coming home. Recently, I had been traveling for five months and was talking to Madison on Skype. I asked her what she wanted for her upcoming birthday and after a long pause… she said, "I just want you to come home." I bought a plane ticket home the next day. While traveling you realize how much that we take for granted when we are home. Traveling to faraway lands without those we love gives them and us an opportunity to realize what life would be without them. Upon returning from our trip, there is a much greater appreciation and understanding of the importance that they play in our life.

> "THE REAL TREASURE FOR WHICH WE ALL SEEK IS NEVER VERY FAR; THERE IS NO REAL NEED TO SEEK IT IN A DISTANT PLACE, FOR IT LIES BURIED WITHIN OUR OWN HEARTS. AND YET, THERE IS THIS STRANGE AND PERSISTENT FACT, THAT IT IS ONLY AFTER A JOURNEY IN A DISTANT REGION, IN A NEW LAND, THAT THE WAY TO THAT TREASURE BECOMES CLEAR."
> *Heinrich Zimmer*

While everything looks the same, it also feels unfamiliar. Something is different and that something is you. After being home for a few days, a calmness comes over you as you settle into your normal routine. There is nothing better than sleeping in your own bed after a long trip. Finally, you have an opportunity to rest without having to make decisions about your next destination such as where to stay and how to get there. And this is great, for a while.

> "A MIND THAT IS STRETCHED BY NEW EXPERIENCES CAN NEVER GO BACK TO ITS OLD DIMENSIONS."
>
> *Anonymous*

Once people stop asking you about your trip, you realize that you don't have anything else to say. Your attempts to share your enthusiasm and memories may be met with indifference, even jealousy, from others. Remember that you have done something that few have had the opportunity to do, so don't take it personally. The purpose of your trip was for your enjoyment, not to impress others. As the days go by and monotony sets in you begin to feel out of place. The urge to travel starts to consume you.

> "ONCE YOU HAVE TRAVELED, THE VOYAGE
> NEVER ENDS, BUT IS PLAYED OUT OVER AND OVER
> AGAIN IN THE QUIETEST CHAMBERS. THE MIND CAN
> NEVER BREAK OFF THE JOURNEY."
>
> *Pat Conroy*

You start planning and searching the web for new travel opportunities. You begin to realize that you have more in common with strangers that you met in a hostel than people you have known for your entire life; due to your shared passion for travel. It becomes more difficult because you cannot understand why everyone does not backpack and why everyone thinks you are a little crazy for doing so.

Writing about your travels either for yourself or for a local paper helps to make the transition back to the real world, whatever that is. Searching out like-minded people who enjoy talking about traveling and keeping in touch with friends you made on previous trips seems to help. Planning that next trip, whenever it may be, seems to give me peace while at home. It is the light at the end of the tunnel.

After much frustration, I finally realized that it is not them but me. I have chosen to be one of the crazed few who will travel anywhere, anytime and for any reason for the sake of traveling. Money and time constraints are a secondary thought. Such is the travel addiction.

"THOSE WHO WANDER ARE NOT NECESSARILY LOST."

J.R.R. Tolkien

While many may backpack for a while and then return to their everyday lives, some will see backpacking as a way of life. It is those serious backpackers who will truly understand this chapter and for whom it was written.

"IN A SENSE, IT'S THE COMING BACK, THE RETURN, WHICH GIVES MEANING TO THE GOING FORTH. WE REALLY DON'T KNOW WHERE WE HAVE BEEN UNTIL WE'VE COME BACK TO WHERE WE WERE. ONLY, WHERE WE WERE MAY NOT BE AS IT WAS BECAUSE OF WHO WE'VE BECOME, WHICH, AFTER ALL, IS WHY WE LEFT."

(Bernard, "Northern Exposure")

Made in the USA
Charleston, SC
02 June 2012